SMUGGLERS MURDERS

*Authentick Transcription of events recorded 1749:
Wherein south coast free-traders, roused by the
Hawkhurst Gang, broke open the Custom-house
at Poole, to rescue their consignment of Tea.*

Written by a GENTLEMAN at Chichester.
First Edition *printed & originally sold by
R Walker in the Little Old Bailey, London
and by several others across the South of England.*
Tenth Edition *published by a gentleman at Hawkhurst.*

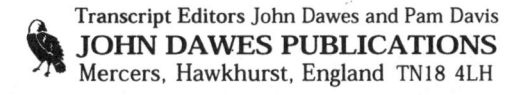

Transcript Editors John Dawes and Pam Davis
JOHN DAWES PUBLICATIONS
Mercers, Hawkhurst, England TN18 4LH

A FULL and GENUINE
HISTORY
Of the Inhuman and Unparellell'd
MURDERS
OF
Mr. WILLIAM GALLEY, a Custom-House
Officer at the Port of Southampton:
And Mr. DANIEL CHATER, a Shoemaker,
at Fordingbridge in Hampshire:
By FOURTEEN Notorious SMUGGLERS.

With the Trials of the seven Bloody Criminals at
Chichester, by virtue of a Special Commission, on the 16th,
17th, and 18th of January, 1748-9, before Mr. Justice Fos-
ter, Mr. Baron Clive, and Mr. Justice Birch.
Also the Trials of John Mills, alias Smoaker, and
Henry Sheerman, alias Little Harry; With an Account of
the wicked Lives of the sd. Henry Sheerman, Lawrence and
Thomas Kemp, two Brothers, Robert Fuller, and Jockey
Brown, condemned at the said Assizes at East Grinstead.
With the Trials at large of Thomas Kingsmill
alias Stay-maker, and other Smugglers, for breaking
the King's Custom-House, at Poole, in Dorsetsh.
TO THE WHOLE IS ADDED,
A Sermon preached in the Cathedral Church
Chichester, at a Special Assize held there January
1748-9, before the Honourable Mr. Justice Foster, &c.

Written by a GENTLEMAN at Chichester

THE THIRD EDITION

LONDON:
Printed for and sold by G. ROBINSON, in Pater-noster-
Row; J. RUSSEL, at Guildford; T. FORDE, at South-
ampton; J. WILKES, at Winchester; J. BREADHOWER,
at Portsmouth; J. GAIST, at Portsmouth Common; W.
STAPLES, at Havant; W. LEE, at Lewes; T. WHITE,
at Arundel; and P. HUMPHRY and W. ARNALIN, in
Chichester. M.DCC.LXXIX.

Title page 3rd edition

British Library Cataloguing in Publication Data
***Smugglers murders: authentick transcription of events recorded 1749: wherein
south coast free-traders, roused by the Hawkhurst Gang, broke open the
Custom House at Poole, to rescue their consignment of tea. – 10th ed.***
　1. Smugglers - England - Poole - History - 18th century
　2. Murderers - England - Poole - History - 18th century
　3. Smuggling - England - Poole - History - 18th century
　4. Murder - England - Poole - History - 18th century
I. Dawes, John II. Davis, Pam
364.1'33

ISBN 0 947685 18 9
Printed by The Book Company at Ipswich.
Cover printed by The Wealden Advertiser at Hawkhurst.
Typeset by Pam Davis in Caslon; originally design'd and cutt 1722.
© 1999 10th Edition John Dawes Publications, Hawkhurst.
All rights reserved. No part of this publication may be reproduced, stored in a retrieval system, or transmitted, in any form or by any means, electronic, mechanical, photocopying, recording or otherwise, without prior permission in writing from the publisher.

TO THE
PUBLICK.

THIS History was first published in 1749, soon after the Execution of Jackson, Carter, and other Smugglers, upon the Broil, near Chichester. The Writer in his Preface, says, 'I do assure the Public, that I took
' down the Facts in Writing from the
' Mouths of the Witnesses; that I fre-
' quently conversed with the Prisoners,
' both before and after Condemnation; by
' which I had an Opportunity of procu-
' ring those Letters which are herein af-
' ter inserted, and other Intelligence of
• some secret Transactions among them,
' which were never communicated to any
' other Person.' Its Authenticity thus shewn, he further says, ' Of all the mon-
' monstrous

' strous Wickednesses with which the Age
' abounds, nothing, I will be bold to say,
' can parellel the Scenes of Villainy that
' are here laid open. In all the Histories
' I have ever read, of all the barbarous
' Stories I have heard related, never did
' I meet with an Instance where Cruelty
' was carried to such an Excess as here.
' We have an Instance of two Men suf-
' fering the most cruel Torments that Ma-
' lice itself could invent, without any Pro-
' vocation given, and for no other Crime
' but a Duty to serve their King and
' Country.

He also says, ' When the Facts were
' proved by undeniable Evidence in the
' Face of the Court, what Horror and
' Detestation appeared in the Countenance
' of every one present! Every one shudder'd
' when they heard the aggravating Cir-
' cumstances of the Murders related, and
' how barbarously the Villains handled their
' two wretched Victims. The Judges
' themselves declar'd on the Bench, that
' in all their Reading, they never met
' with such a continued Scene of Barba-
' rity, so deliberately carried on, and so
' cruelly

' *cruelly executed.* The Council, Jury,
' and all present were astonish'd and shock'd
' to hear prov'd, beyond Contradiction,
' Facts of so monstrous a Nature, as the
' Sufferings were of Mr. Chater and Mr.
' Galley.

' But how monstrous and unnatual so-
' ever the Facts here related appear, yet
' they are certainly true ; every Thing is
' related just in the Manner it was acted,
' without the least Aggravation to set it
' off. I have set down nothing but what the
' Witnesses themselves declared upon their
' Oaths, except in some few Circumstances
' which Steele declar'd on his first Exami-
' nation, but was not examined on his
' Trial. And therefore, upon the Whole,
' I affirm, that the following Account is
' genuine and authentick,

A Reverend Writer says, ' In order to
' deter Mankind from the Perpetration of
' notorious Crimes, nothing can be so effec-
' tual as to represent, in the most striking
' Colours, the Punishments that naturally
' attend them. The Fear of Shame as
' often preserves a Person from the Com-
' mission

' mission of a Crime, as the Expectation
' of a Reward for his continuing in the
' Paths of Virtue.' Mr. POPE *also says*,

' VICE is a *Monster* of such frightful Mien,
' As, to be hated, needs but to be seen.'

These Authorities, 'tis hoped, will be a sufficient Apology for reprinting the said History ; and as the chief Motive thereto is that of serving the Community, the Editors humbly hope it will meet with due Encouragement, more especially, as such Republication may justly be considered as one Means (amongst many others) of checking that audacious Spirit which now [December 1779] *dayly gains Ground, by reminding those Violaters of the Laws, that, like Jackson and the other Miscreants mentioned in this Work, they will most assuredly receive that just Punishment their Crimes merit, if they continue their unlawful and wicked Practices. On the other Hand, did they seriously consider the dreadful Consequences which frequently follow, they would shudder to think of them ; they would at once see and confess their own Unworthiness ; they would be thoroughly sensible, that to answer the Purposes of their Great Creator,*

[vii]

Creator, they should use their utmost Endeavors to get an honest Livelihood in the several Stations to which they may respectively be called; they would then be useful Members of the Community; and by such Conduct would avoid those dreadful Horrors and most bitter Pangs which for ever haunt guilty Minds.

The better to attain these most desirable and salutary Ends, Parents, Guardians, and others who have the Tuition of Youth (we mean here the Youth of the Poor and the Illiterate in general), should now and then take Occasion to read, or cause to be read, to their Servants, &c. divers Passages of this true History; at the same Time make such Remarks, and draw such Inferences from them, as their own natural good Sense and Experience might point out; and more especially they should put them in Mind, that GOD, *by the Mouth of his Servant* MOSES, *expressly declares,* He who sheddeth Man's Blood, by Man shall his Blood be shed.

' *I have drawn it up in the Way of a*
' *Narrative, as the best Method of giving*
a

'a full View of the Whole Affair. When
'that is over, I proceed to give an Ac-
'count of their Trials; after which I con-
'clude with their Lives, Confessions, Be-
'haviour, and last dying Words at the
'Place of Execution.

'I cannot omit mentioning here, that

'Mr. Banks made a Speech exceeding
'eloquent and judicious, which drew the
'Attention of the whole Court; and
'which he concluded with that wise Say-
'ing of the wisest of Men, That the Mer-
'cies of the Wicked are Cruelties. The
'Truth of which will evidently appear in
'the following Pages.

A

[1]

A Full and Genuine

HISTORY

OF THE

INHUMAN MURDERS

OF

William Galley and *Daniel Chater*, &c.

IN September 1747, one John Diamond, otherwise Dymar, agreed with a Number of Smugglers, to go over to the Island of Guernsey, to smuggle Tea ; where having purchas'd a considerable Quantity, on their Return in a Cutter, were taken by one Capt. Johnson, who carried the Vessel and Tea to the Port of Pool, and lodg'd the Tea in the Custom-House there.

The Smugglers being very much incens'd at this fatal Miscarriage of their Purchase, resolve not to sit down contented with the Loss ; but, on a Consultation held among them, they agreed to go and take away the Tea from the

B   Warehouse

Warehouse where it was lodg'd. Accordingly, the Beginning of the next Month, a Body of them, to the Number of sixty, well arm'd, assembled in Charlton Forest, and from thence proceeded on their Enterprize; to accomplish which, they agreed, that only thirty of them should go upon the Attack, and that the remaining thirty should be placed as Scouts upon the different Roads, to watch the Motions of the Officers and Soldiers, and to be ready to assist or alarm the main Body, in Case any Opposition should be made.

In the Night-time, between the 6th and 7th of October, they went to Pool, about thirty only present, broke open the Custom-house, and took away all the said Tea, except one Bag of about five Pounds.

The next Morning, they return'd with their Booty thro' Fordingbridge in Hampshire, where some Hundreds of People were assembled to view the Cavalcade. Among the Spectators was Daniel Chater, a Shoemaker, (one of the unhappy Persons murder'd) known to Diamond, one of the Gang then passing, as having formerly work'd together in Harvest Time. Diamond shook Hands with him as he pass'd along, and threw him a Bag of Tea.

His Majesty's Proclamation coming out, with a Promise of Reward for apprehending those Persons who were concern'd in breaking open the Custom-house at Pool, and Diamond being

being taken into Custody at Chichester, on a Suspicion of being one of them, and Chater saying, in Conversation with his Neighbours, that he knew Diamond, and saw him go by with the Gang, the Day after the Custom-house at Pool was broke open, it came to the Knowledge of Mr. Shearer, Collector of the Customs at the Port of Southampton, when after some Things that pass'd by Letter, between him and Chater, he was order'd to send Mr. William Galley, (the other unfortunate Person murder'd) with Chater, with a Letter to Major Battin, a Justice of Peace for the County of Sussex, the Purport of which was, to desire the Justice to take an Examination of Chater, in relation to what he knew of that Affair ; and whether he could prove the Identity of Diamond's Person.

On Sunday the 14th of February they set out; and going for Chichester, they call'd at Mr. Holton's at Havant, who was an Acquaintance of Chater's ; Holton ask'd Chater where they were going, and Chater told him they were going to Chichester, to carry a Letter to Major Battin ; when Mr. Holton told him the Major was at East Marden, near Chichester, and directed him and Galley to go by Stanstead, near Rowland's Castle. Galley and Chater pursuing their Journey, and going thro' Leigh, in the Parish of Havant, in their Way to Rowland's Castle, they call'd at the new Inn, and asking the nearest Way, they saw Mr. Geo. Austin, and Mr. Tho. Austin, two Brothers, and their Brother-in-law

[4]

Mr. Jenkes; when the elder Brother G. Austin said, they were going the same Way, and would shew them; and they all set out together (Galley, Chater, and the rest being all on Horseback:) And about 12 at Noon came to the White-Hart at Rowland's Castle, a House kept by one Elizabeth Payne, Widow, who had two Sons, both Men grown, and Blacksmiths, and reputed Smugglers, in the same Village. After calling for some Rum, Mrs. Payne took Mr. George Austin aside, and told him she was afraid these two Strangers were come with an Intent to do some Injury to the Smugglers. He replied, he believ'd she need be under no such Apprehension on that Account, for they were only carrying a Letter to Major Battin; and as he did not know the Purport of it, he imagin'd it was only about some common Business. The Circumstance, however, of their having a Letter for the Major, increas'd her Suspicion: Upon which she sent one of her Sons, who was then in the House, for William Jackson and William Carter, two of the Murderers, (as will appear hereafter) who liv'd within a small Distance of her House. While her Son was gone, Chater and Galley wanted to be going, and ask'd for their Horses; but Mrs. Payne told them, that the Man was gone out with the Key of the Stables, and would be at Home presently, which Words she said in order to keep them till Jackson and Carter, or both came, who liv'd very near.

As

As soon as Jackson came in, who was there first, he order'd a Pot of Hot to be made, and while that was getting ready Carter came in ; Mrs. Payne immediately took them aside, and told them her Suspicions concerning Chater and Galley, and likewise the circumstance of a Letter which they were carrying to Major Battin, and soon after advis'd Geo. Austin, to go away about his Business, telling him, as she respected him, he had better go, and not stay, lest he should come to some Harm ; upon which he went away, and left his Brother Thomas and Brother-in-law Mr. Jenkes there.

During this Time, Mrs. Payne's other Son came in, and finding there were Grounds to suspect, that the two Strangers were going to make Information against the Smugglers, he went out and fetch'd in William Steele, (who was one of the King's Witnesses upon Trial) and Samuel Downer, otherwise Samuel Howard, otherwise Little Sam, Edmund Richards, Henry Sheerman, otherwise Little Harry, all Smugglers, and all belonging to the same Gang, and were indicted for the Murder of Mr. Galley, but not then taken.

After they had drank a little while, Jackson took Chater into the Yard, and ask'd him how he did, and where Diamond was ; Chater said, he believ'd he was in Custody, but how he did he did not know ; but that he was going to appear against him, which he was sorry for, but could not help it. Galley soon after came into

into the Yard to them, to get Chater in again, suspecting that Jackson was persuading Chater not to persist in giving Information against the Smugglers, and upon Galley's desiring Chater to come in, Jackson said, *G—d d————n your B————d, what is that to you?* strikes him a Blow in the Face, and knocks him down, and set his Nose and Mouth a bleeding ; after which they all came into the House, Jackson abusing Galley ; when Galley said he was the King's Officer, and could not put up with such Usage ; then Jackson replied, *You a King's Officer! I'll make a King's Officer of you; and for a Quartern of Gin I'll serve you so again ;* and some Time after offering to strike him again, one of the Payne's interpos'd, and said, *Don't be such a Fool, do you know what you are doing ?*

Galley and Chater began to be very uneasy, and wanted to be going ; upon which Jackson, Carter, and the rest of them, persuaded them to stay and drink more Rum, and make it up, for they were sorry for what had happen'd, when they all sat down together, Mr. Austin and Mr. Jenkes being present. After they had sat a little while, Jackson and Carter wanted to see the Letter which Galley and Chater where carrying to Major Battin's, but they refus'd to shew it ; upon which they both made a Resolution that they would see it. They then drank about pretty plentifully, and made Galley, Chater, and Tho. Austin fuddled ; when they persuaded Galley and Chater to go into
another

another Room, where there was a Bed, and lie down ; which they did, and fell asleep ; and then the Letter was taken out of one of their Pockets, and brought into the Kitchen, where Carter or Kelly read it ; and the Contents of it being plainly a Design to promote an Information against some of their Gang, they immediately enter'd into a Consultation what Course to take on this Occasion. Some proposed one Thing, some another; but they all agreed in this, that the Letter should be first destroy'd, and then they would consider what to do with the Men, in order to prevent their giving the intended Information.

Before this, one John Race, (who was also one of the King's Witnesses) and Richard Kelly came in, when Jackson and Carter told them, they had got the old Rogue the Shoemaker of Fordingbridge, who was going to give an Information against John Diamond, the Shepherd, who was then in Custody at Chichester. Then they all consulted what was best to be done with him and Galley, when William Steele proposed to take them both to a Well, a little way from the House, and to murder them, and throw them in.

At this Consultation were present only these seven Smugglers, namely Wm. Jackson, Wm. Carter, Wm. Steele, John Race, Samuel Downer, Edmund Richards, and Henry Sheerman, and this Proposal was disagreed to, as they had been seen in their Company by the Austins

[8]

stins, Mr. Jenkes, Mr. Garrat, Mr. Poate, and others who came into Payne's House to drink. This being disagreed to, another Proposal was made, which was, to take them away, and send them over to France; but that was object'd against, as there was a Possibility of their coming over again, and then they should be all known. At these Consultations Jackson's and Carter's Wives were both present, and who both cried out, *Hang the Dogs, for they came here to hang us.* Then another Proposition was made, which was that they would take them, and carry them to some Place where they should be confined, till it was known what would be the Fate of Diamond, and in the mean Time each of them to allow three Pence a Week to subsist Galley and Chater; and that whatever Diamond's Fate was, they determined that theirs should be the same.

Galley and Chater continued all this while asleep upon the Bed; then Jackson went in and began the first Scene of their Cruelty; for having first put on his Spurs, he got upon the Bed and Spurr'd their Foreheads to wake them, and then afterwards whipp'd them with a Horsewhip; so that when they came out into the Kitchen, Chater was as bloody as Galley. This done all the abovesaid Smugglers being present, they took them out of the House, when Richards with a Pistol cock'd in his Hand, swore he would shoot any Person through

Mr. Galley and Mr. Chater put by ye Smugglers on one Horse near Rowland Castle.
A. Steele who was Admitted a Kings Evidence. B. Little Harry. C. Jackson. D Carter.
E. Downer. F. Richards. 1. Mr. Galley. 2. Mr. Chater.

through the Head that should mention any Thing of what was done, or what they had heard.

When they were all come out of the House, Jackson return'd with a Pistol in his Hand, and ask'd for a Belt, a Strap, or String ; but none of the People in the House presumed to give him either ; upon which he returned to the rest of the Gang, who were lifting Galley on a Horse, whose Legs they tied under the Horse's Belly ; then they lifted Chater on the same Horse, and tied his Legs under the Horse's Belly, and then tied their four Legs together.

All this Time John Race was with them ; but when they began to set forward, Race said, I can't go with you, for I have never a Horse, and so staid behind.

They had not gone above 100 Yards before Jackson call'd out, *Whip 'em, cut 'em, slash 'em, damn 'em ;* and then all fell upon them, except the Person who was leading the Horse, which was Steel ; for the Roads were so bad that they were forced to go very slow.

They whipp'd them till they came to *Wood's Ashes,* some with long Whips, some with short, lashing and cutting them over the Head, Face, Eyes, Shoulders, or wherever they could injure them most, and continued this terrible Exercise till the poor Men, unable any longer to bear the smarting Anguish of their repeated Blows, rolled from Side to Side, and at last

last fell together with their Heads under the Horse's Belly; in which Posture every Step the Horse made he struck one or the other of their Heads with his Feet. This happened at *Wood's Ashes*, as I have said before, which was more than half a Mile from the Place where they began their Whipping, and had continued it all the Way thither. When their cruel Tormentors saw the dismal Effects of their Barbarity, and that the poor Creatures were fallen under it, they set 'em upright again in the same Position as they were before, and continued whipping them in the most cruel Manner over the Head, Face, Shoulders, and every where, till they came beyond *Goodthrop Dean,* upwards of half a Mile farther, the Horse still going a very slow Pace; where they both fell again as before, with their Heads under the Horse's Belly, and their Heels up in the Air.

Now they found them so weak, that they could not sit upon the Horse at all, upon which they separated them, and put Galley behind Steel, and Chater behind Little Sam, and then whipp'd Galley so severely, that the Lashes coming upon Steel, he desir'd them to desist, crying out himself, that he could not bear it, upon which they desisted accordingly. All the Time they so continued to whip them, Jackson rode with a Pistol cock'd, and swore as they went along through Dean, if they made any Noise he would blow their Brains out. They then agreed to go up with them

to

Galley & Chater *falling off their Horse at Woodash, draggs thier Heads on the Ground, while the Horse kicks them as he goes; the Smugglers still continuing thier brutish Usage.*

to Harris's Well, near Lady-Holt Park, where they swore they would murder Galley; accordingly they took him off the Horse, and threatened to throw him into the Well. Upon which the poor unhappy Man desir'd them to dispatch him at once, or even throw him down the Well, to put an End to his Misery. *No, G—d d——n your Blood,* says Jackson, *if that's the Case, we must have something more to say to you*; and then put him upon a Horse again, and whipp'd him over the Downs, till he was so weak, that he fell off.

Was ever Cruelty like this! What? deny a miserable Wretch, who was half dead with their Blows and Bruises, the wretched Favour of a quick Dispatch out of his Tortures! Could the Devil himself have furnish'd a more execrable Invention to punish the wretched Victims of his Malice, than to grant them Life only to prolong their Torments?

Poor Galley not being able to sit a Horseback any longer, Carter and Jackson took him up, and laid him across the Saddle, with his Breast over the Pomel, as a Butcher does a Calf, and Richards got up behind him to hold him, and after carrying him in this Manner above a Mile, Richards was tir'd of holding him, so let him down by the Side of the Horse; and then Carter and Jackson put him upon the grey Horse that Steel had before rode upon: They set him up with his Legs across the Saddle, and his Body over the Horse's Mane;

and in this Posture Jackson held him on for half a Mile, most of the Way the poor Man cried out, *Barbarous Usage! barbarous Usage! for God's Sake shoot me thro' the Head*; Jackson all the Time squeezing his private Parts.

After going on in this Manner upwards of a Mile, Little Harry tied Galley with a Cord, and got up behind him, to hold him from falling off ; and when they had gone a little Way, in that Manner, the poor Man, Galley, cried out, *I fall, I fall I fall* ; and Little Harry giving him a Shove as he was falling, said *Fall and be d——n'd* : Upon which he fell down, and Steel said that they all thought he had broke his Neck, and was dead : But it must be presum'd that he was buried alive, because when he was found, his Hands cover'd his Face, as if to keep the Dirt out of his Eyes.

Poor unhappy Galley! Who can read the melancholy Story of thy tragical Catastrophe without shedding Tears at the sorrowful Relation? What Variety of Pains did thy Body feel in every Member of it, especially by thy Privy Parts being so us'd? What Extremity of Anguish didst thou groan under, so long as the small Remains of Life permitted thee to be sensible of it? And, after all, to be buried while Life was yet in thee, and to struggle with Death even in thy wretched Grave, what Imagination can form to itself a Scene of greater Horror, or more detestable Villainy? Sure thy Murderers must be Devils incarnate! For none but the

the Fiends of Hell could take Pleasure in the Torments of two unhappy Men, who had given them no Offence, unless their endeavouring to serve their King and Country may be deemed such. This indeed was the Plea of these vile Miscreants ; but a very bad Plea it was to support as bad a Cause. But such is the Depravity of human Nature, that when a Man once abandons himself to all Manner of Wickedness, he sets no Bounds to his Passions, his Conscience is fear'd, every tender Sentiment is lost, Reason is no more, and he has nothing left him of a Man but the Form.

We forgot to mention, in its proper Place, that in order to make their Whipping the more severly felt, they pulled off Galley's Great Coat, which was found in the Road the next Morning all bloody.

They supposing Galley was dead, laid him cross a Horse, two of the Smugglers, one on each Side, holding him to prevent his falling off, while a third led the Horse, and as they were going up a dirty Lane, Jackson said, *Stop at the Swing Gate beyond the Water, till we return, and we will go and seek for a Place to carry them both to ;* when he and Carter went to the House of one Pescod, who had been a reputed Smuggler, and knocking at the Door, the Daughter came down, when they said they had got two Men whom they wanted to bring to the House. The Girl told them her Father was ill, and had been so for some Time, and that

that there was no Conveniency for them, nor any Body to look after them; and they insisting that she should go up and ask him, she did, and brought down Word, that her Father would suffer no Body to be brought there, be they who they would; upon which they return'd to the rest.

Tho' this Pescod was (as I have observ'd) a reputed Smuggler, and therefore these Fellows suppos'd he would give them Harbour upon this Occasion, yet it does not appear that he had gone such Lengths as the rest of them had done; for if he had, he would not have refus'd admitting them at any Hour of the Night, notwithstanding his Illness; but he imagining they were upon some villaneous Expedition, resolv'd to have no Hand in it, or have his Name brought in Question on that Account. But to proceed.

By this Time it was between 1 and 2 in the Morning, when they agreed to go to one Scardefield's at the Red Lion at Rake, which was not far from them. When they came there, they knock'd at the Door, but the Family being all in Bed, Scardefield look'd out of the Window, and ask'd who was there. Carter and Jackson told him who they were, and desir'd him to get up, for they wanted something to drink, and that there were more Company coming: Scardefield refus'd several Times, but they pressing him very hard, he put on his Cloaths, and came down, and let them in after many Times refusing.

As

As soon as he was down, and had let Steel, Jackson, Carter, and Richards in, he made a Fire in the Parlour, and then went to draw some Liquor, which while he was doing he heard more Company come in ; and he going into his Brewhouse, saw something lie upon the Ground, like a dead Man. They then sent him to fetch 'em some Rum, and some Gin, and while he was gone for the same, they had got poor Chater into the Parlour, and on his bringing the Liquor they refus'd to admit him in, but he saw a Man, he says, stand up very bloody, whom he suppos'd to be Chater. They told him, Scardefield, that they had an Engagement with some Officers, and had lost their Tea, and were afraid that several of their People were kill'd ; which they probably said, as well to conceal their Murder of Galley, as to account for Chater's being bloody.

All this Time poor Mr. Chater was in Expectation, every Moment, of being kill'd ; and indeed when I am speaking of it, my Heart bleeds for his Sufferings ; but they sent him now out of the Way, for Jackson and Little Harry carry'd him down to old Mills's, which was not far off, and then return'd again to the Company.

After they had drank pretty plentifully, they all went out, taking Galley, or his Corpse, if he was quite dead, with them ; when Carter and Richards return'd to Scardefield's and ask'd him if he could find the Place out where they
had

[16]

had some time before lodg'd some Goods ; and he said he believ'd he could, but could not go then, but Richards & Carter insisted he should; and then Carter took a Candle and Lanthorn, and borrow'd a Spade, and they went together, and had not gone far before they came to the rest, who were waiting ; and then Scardefield saw something lie cross a Horse, which he thought look'd like the dead Body of a Man ; and that Little Sam having a Spade, began to dig a Hole, and it being a very cold Morning, he help'd, but did know what it was for ; and in this Hole they buried poor Mr. Galley.

They then return'd to Scardefield's, and sat carousing the best Part of Monday, having as Jackson told them, secur'd Chater.

This Scardefield was formerly thought to have been concern'd with the Smugglers ; — and as he kept a publick House, they thought they might take any Liberties with him. And it seems evident, by what they did after they had gain'd Admission, for they only wanted a covenient Place, to consult at Leisure what Course to pursue on this Occasion. They had two Prisoners, one of whom they suppos'd they had already murder'd, whose Body they must dispose of in some Manner or other. The other, though yet living, they resolv'd should undergo the same Fate, but by what Means it does not appear they had yet agreed. The better to blind Scardefield, whom they did not care

to

William Galley, brought cross a Horse to a Sand Pit where a deep Hole is Dug to Bury him in.

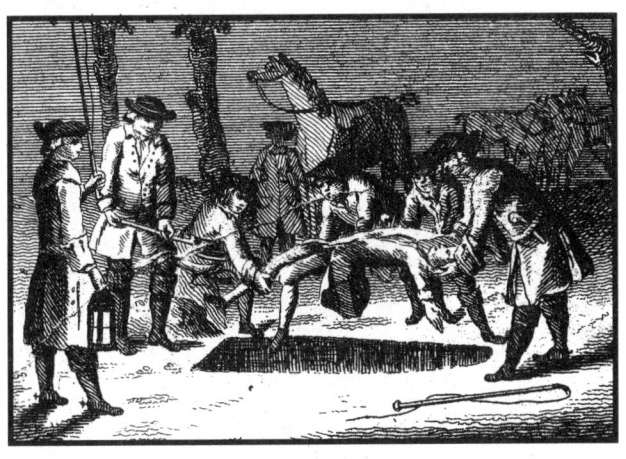

The unfortunate William Galley put by the Smugglers into the Ground & as is generally believed before he was quite DEAD.

to let into the Secret of their bloody Scheme, and likewise to give some colourable Pretence for what his own Eyes had been Witness to, (a dead Corpse in his Brewhouse, and a Man all over bloody standing in his Parlour) they tell him a plausible Story of an Engagement they had with the King's Officers. Now, whether Scardefield gave entire Credit to what they told him or whether he really suspected what they were upon, did not appear from the Evidence. This, however, is certain, that he went with them to the Place, and assisted them in burying the Body of Galley; and therefore one would imagine he could not be entirely ignorant of what they were doing. But as he was one of the Witnesses, by which this Scene of Iniquity was brought to Light, and as he was likewise a Person of a tolerable good Character, we shall forbear saying any Thing that may seem to throw a Slur on his Reputation.

But now we must return to the melancholy Story of the unfortunate Man, unhappy in the Hands of the most cruel Wretches surely ever breathing.

While they were sitting at Scardefield's, consulting together what they were to do next, Richard Mills came by: This Richard was the Son of old Richard Mills, to whose House they had convey'd Chater for his better Security, till they had resolv'd what to do with him. When they saw young Mills, they call'd him in, in, and related to him in what manner they had treated Chater, who was going to make an Information against their Friend Diamond the Shepherd, and that in their Way they came by a Precipice 30 Foot deep. To this Mills made Answer, that if he had been there, he would have call'd a Council of War, and thrown him down headlong. So that it seems as if Cruelty was the ruling Principle among the whole Body of Smugglers, and that nothing less than the Death or Destruction of all those they deem'd their Adversaries, that is, all such as endeavour'd to prevent or interrupt them in the pernicious Trade of Smuggling, would content 'em.

They continued drinking at Scardefield's all that Day, which was Monday, Chater being chain'd all the while by the Leg, with an Iron Chain about three Yards long, in a Place belonging to old Mills, call'd a Skilling, which is what they lay Turf up in, and look'd after by Little Harry and old Mills : and in the dead of that Night they agreed to go home separately, and to rally up some more of their Gang, and to meet at Scardefield's on Wednesday.

Their Design in this was, that they might appear at their own Homes on Tuesday Mornng early, so that their Neighbours might have no Suspicion of what they had been about, or of what they had still in Hand to do, and likewise to consult with the rest of their Gang, what was best to be done.

They

[19]

They all met at Scardefield's on Wednesday Evening, according to Appointment ; that is, William Jackson, William Carter, Wm. Steel, (one of the King's Witnesses) Edmund Richards of Long Coppice in the Parish of Warblington, in the County of Sussex, and Samuel Howard, otherwise Little Sam, of Rowland's Castle, in the County of Hants, who were five of the Six concern'd in the Murder of Galley, as has been before related. Also John Cobby, William Hammond, Benjamin Tapner, Tho. Stringer of the City of Chichester, Cordwainer, Daniel Perryer, otherwise Little Daniel of Norton, and John Mills of Trotton, both in the County of Sussex ; and Thomas Willis, commonly call'd the Coachman of Selbourne, near Liphook, in the County of Hants, Richard Mills, jun. and John Race, another King's Witness, being 14 in Number : Richard Mills sen. and Henry Sheerman, alias Little Harry, staid at Home to take Care of Chater, in whose Custody they had left him. They dropt in one after another, as if by Accident, so that it was late in the Night before they were all got together. Being all of them at last come in, they enter'd upon the Business for which they were then met, namely, to consult cooly and sedately what was to be done with Chater, that is, how to dispatch him in such a Manner as would be least liable to Discovery ; for, that he must be destroy'd, had been already unanimously detemin'd, as the only Method they could

could think of to prevent his telling Tales about Galley. Thus when a Course of Villainy is once begun, it is impossible to say where it will end; one Crime brings on another, and that treads on the Heels of a third, till at length both the Innocent and the Guilty are swept away into the Gulph of Destruction.

I cannot pass in Silence, without making Mention of the Readiness old Mills shew'd when they brought poor Chater first down to his House; for he fetch'd out of a Pantry both Victuals and Drink, when they all eat and drank, except Chater, who could not eat, but vomited very much.

After they had debated the Matter some Time among them, Richard Mills jun. propos'd this Method: As Chater is already chain'd fast to a Post, let us, said he, load a Gun with two or three Bullets, then lay it upon a Stand, with the Muzzle of the Piece levell'd at his Head, and after having tied a long String to the Trigger, we will all go to the Butt End, and each of us taking hold of the String, pull it together; thus we shall be all equally guilty of his Death, and it will be impossible for any one of us to charge the rest with his Murder, without accusing himself of the same Crime; and none can pretend to lessen or mitigate their Guilt, by saying they were only Accessaries, since all will be Principals. But some, more infernally barbarous than the rest, (but who, the Witness Steele
                                                could

could not recollect) objected to this Proposal, as too expeditious a Method of dispatching him, and that it would put him out of his Misery too soon; for they were resolv'd he should suffer as much, and as long as they could make his Life last, as a Terror to all such informing Rogues (as they term'd it) for the future.

This Proposal being rejected, another was offer'd and agreed to, and that was, to go to old Major Mills, as he was call'd, and fetch him away from thence, and carry him up to Harris's Well, near Lady-Holt Park, and throw him in there, as they intended to have done by Galley, as the most effectual Method to secrete the Murder from the Knowlege of the World; forgetting that the Eye of Providence was constantly upon them, watch'd all their Motions, and would certainly, one Day or other, bring to light their Deeds of Darkness; and that Divine Justice never forgets the Cries of the Oppressed, but will, in due Time, retaliate the Cruelties exercis'd on the Innocent, on the Heads of their inexorable Tyrants and Tormentors.

All this while the unhappy Chater remain'd in the most deplorable Situation that ever miserable Wretch was confin'd to; his Mind full of Horror, and his Body all over Pain and Anguish with the Blows and Scourges they had given him, and every Moment in Expectation of worse Treatment than he had yet met with,

without

without any Sustenance to support his wretched Life than now and then a little Bread and Water, and once some Peas Porridge. Besides all this, he was continually visited by one or other of them, who remain'd at the House, not to comfort or relieve him with Words of Kindness, or Promises of better Usage, not to refresh him with Cordials, or agreeable Nourishment, but to renew their cruel Exercise of beating and abusing him, and to swear and upbraid him in the vilest Terms, and the most scurrilous Language that their Tongues could utter.

Having at length concluded what to do with their poor unhappy Prisoner, they all went down to old Mills's, where they immediately open'd a fresh Scene of Barbarity. For as soon as they came in, Tapner, Cobby, and some others of them, went directly into the Turf-House, where they found Chater in the most piteous Condition, enough to melt a Heart, not made of Stone, into Compassion; but was so far from moving the Pity of these merciless Bloodhounds, that it only serv'd them as a fresh Motive to renew their Cruelties, and aggravate his Afflictions. Tapner, in particular, immediately pull'd out a large Clasp Knife, and express'd himself in this horrible manner: *G—d d———n your Bl———d, down on your Knees, and go to Prayers, for with this Knife I will be your Butcher.* The poor Man, being terrified at this dreadful Menace, and expecting that every Moment would be his last, knelt down upon

Chater, Chained in y^e Turff House at Old Mills's, Cobby, kicking him & Tapner, cutting him Cross y^e Eyes & Nose, while he is saying the Lords Prayer. Several of y^e other Smugglers standing by.

upon a Turf, as he was order'd, and lifted up his Heart and Hands to Heaven, in the best Manner that his Pains and Anguish would suffer him, and while he was thus piously offering up his his Prayers to GOD, Cobby got behind him and kick'd him, and with the most bitter Taunts upbraided him for being an Informing Villain. Chater suffer'd all his Torments with great Patience and Resignation ; and tho' there was scarce a Limb or Joint of him free from the most excruciating Pains, yet, in the midst of all he did not forget his Friend Galley, and believing that he was either dead, or very near it, he begg'd they would tell him what they had done with him. Tapner replied, *D——n you, we have kill'd him, and we will do so by you* ; and then, without more ado, or any other Provocation, as was fully prov'd by the Witnesses on the Trial, drew his Knife aslant over his Eyes and Nose, with such Violence, that he almost cut both his Eyes out, and the Gristle of his Nose quite through. Poor Chater was absolutely at his Mercy, for it was not in his Power to make any Resistance; his great and only Comfort was that he suffer'd in a righteous Cause, and supported with this Consideration, he resign'd himself to the Will of Heaven, which, he was persuaded, took Cognizance of his Sufferings, and would reward his Tormentors according to their Demerits.

Tapner,

Tapner, however, not satisfied with this wanton Act of Cruelty, in another sudden Fit of Phrenzy, aimed another Stroke at his Face, designing to cut him again in the same Wound; but happening to strike a little higher, made a terrible Gash across his Forehead, from which the Blood flowed in Abundance. What a lamentable Figure must this poor Creature make! His Face deeply furrow'd with the most ghastly Wounds, his Eyes cut almost out of his Head, and the Blood running down in Torrents upon the rest of his Body. What a Spectacle was here! yet not miserable enough to move the Compassion of these blood-thirsty Tygers! Old Mills however, not from any Pity, or that his Heart relented at the terrible Condition of this deplorable Object, but apprehending bad Consequences to himself, in Case he should die under their Hands, under his Roof, said to them, *Take him away, and don't murder him here, but murder him somewhere else.*

'Tis surprizing, that this poor miserable Man, who was far advanced in Years, had Strength and Vigour enough to sustain such a Variety of Torments, which the cruel Tyrants inflicted upon him, almost without Intermission, for several Days successively; yet even after this last Act of Barbarity, he had more severe Trials to come before he was suffer'd to part with his wearisome Life. And as the last Scene of this woeful Tragedy appears

more

more astonishing and more monstrous than any Thing they had hitherto transacted, which one would think was almost impossible, we shall give a very particular and circumstantial Account of every Thing that was done on this sad Occasion.

Being all agreed in the Measures they were about to take, they mounted Chater on a Horse, and so set out together for Harris's Well. Mills, however, and his two Sons staid behind, desiring to be excused, because their Horses were not in the Way, or they would very readily have bore them Company on this Occasion if they could, for they were as hearty in the same Cause as the best of them. Beides there was no great Necessity for their Assistance, since there were enough of them, as the Mills's said, to kill one Man; and as Harris's Well lay just in their Way Homewards, the Execution would be little or no Hindrance or Interruption to them in their Journey.

Every Thing being now settled and adjusted, they proceeded on towards the Well. Tapner however more cruel, if possible, than the rest of his bloody Gang, fell to whipping poor Chater again with all his Might over his Face and Eyes, and made his Wounds, which he had before given him with his murdering Knife, bleed afresh; and what is still more amazing, swore, *That if he blooded his Saddle,* (for it seems Chater was set upon his Horse) *he would destroy him that Moment, and send his Soul to Hell :* Which is such an unparellelled Instance of Barbarity, that one would think it impossible that there should be a Creature living, that pretends to Reason, and would be rank'd among Men, could be guilty of. What ! to threaten to murder a Man for a Thing which was not in his Power to avoid, and which the Villain himself was the sole Occasion of ! Horrible, shocking Wickedness ! But let us proceed in our melancholy Story.

At last poor Chater, in this disfigur'd lamentable Condition, is brought to the Well. By that Time they got there, it was the very Dead of Night, and so near the Middle of it, that it was uncertain whether it was Wednesday Night, or Thursday Morning. The Well was between twenty and thirty Foot deep, without Water, and paled round at a small Distance, to keep the Cattle from falling in. Being come up to the Pales, they dismounted Chater, and Tapner taking a Cord out of his Pocket, which he had brought for that Purpose, made a Noose in it, and then fasten'd it round his Neck. This being done, they bade him get over the Pales to the Well. The poor Man observing a small Opening, where a Pale or two had been broken away, made an Attempt to go through ; but that was a Favour too great to be allow'd to so a heinous an Offender, as it seems poor Chater was in their Opinion ; and therefore

Chater hanging at the Well in LADY HOLT Park. the Bloody Villains standing by

The Bloody Smugglers flinging down Stones after they had flung his Dead Body into the Well.

fore one of them swore he should get over, in the Condition he was, and with the Rope about his Neck, all over bloody, his Wounds gaping, and himself extremely weak, and ready to faint thro' Loss of Blood ; yet in this miserable Plight these cruel Executioners oblig'd him to get over the Pales as well as he could.

With a great deal of Difficulty he got over the Pales, when he found himself just upon the Brink of the Well, the Pales standing very near to it. Being over, Tapner took hold of the Rope which was fasten'd to Chater's Neck, and tied it to the Rail of the Pales where the Opening was, for the Well had neither Kirb, Lid, nor Roller. When the Rope was thus fix'd to the Rail, they all got over to him, and push'd him into the Well ; but the Rope being of no great Length, would not suffer his Body to hang lower than Knee-deep in it ; so that the rest of his Body, from his Knees upwards, appear'd above the Well, bending towards the Pales, being held in that Position by the Rope that was tied to the Rail. But as in this Posture he hung leaning against the Side of the Well, the Weight of his Body was not of sufficient Force to strangle him presently. For his inhuman Executioners, whether wearied with tormenting him so long, or whether they wanted to get Home to their several Places, we can't say, but they seem now resolv'd to dispatch him as soon as they could.

E 2   After

After they had waited about a Quarter of an Hour, and perceiv'd by the Struggles he made, that he would be a considerable Time in dying, they alter'd the Method of his Execution. Thomas Stringer, therefore, with the Assistance of Cobby and Hammond, pull'd his Legs out of the Well, and Tapner untying the Cord that was fasten'd to the Rail, his Head fell down upon the Ground, and then bringing it round to the Well, put it in. Then Stringer, who had hold of his Legs, asssisted by Cobby and Hammond, let them go and the Body fell Head foremost into the Well.

Now one would think they had intirely finished their Tragedy, and that this miserable Creature was quite out of his Misery, and beyond the Reach of any further Injury. No, he had yet some further Remains of Life in him, and while he had any Sense left, he must feel the Exercise of their Cruelty.

After they had thrown the Body into the Well, they stood by it some Time ; and it being the dead of the Night, and every Thing still, they heard him breathe or groan, and from thence being assured that he was still alive, and that if they should leave him in that Condition, somebody accidentally passing that Way might possibly hear him ; and in that Case, if the Man should be relieved and brought to Life again, the Consciousness of their own horrid Crimes, and the enormous Barbarities they had exercised upon him and
Galley

Galley, told them that they would certainly be discovered, and then they knew they were dead Men.

Upon which they immediately came to a Resolution to procure a long Ladder that should reach to the Bottom of the Well, and one of them would go down by it and dispatch him at once. Accordingly they went to William Combleach, a Gardener, who lived but a little Way off, and knock'd him up, telling him that one of their Companions was fallen into Harris's Well, and begg'd the Favour he would lend them a Ladder and a Rope to get him out again. Combleach knowing nothing more of the Matter but what they had told him, and thinking he should do a Friendly and Charitable Action, lent them a Ladder, and they carried it away to the Well. Having brought it up to the Pales, whether through the Surprise and Confusion they were in, or the Dread and Horror that might have seiz'd their Minds at that Juncture from the Consideration of the dreadful Work they were about, or from what other Cause is uncertain, they had not all of them Power sufficient to raise the Ladder high enough to get it over the Pales, it being a very long one, tho' there were six of them employed in doing it, namely, Stringer, Steel, Perryer, Hammond, Cobby, and Tapner.

When they had tried some Time, and found all their Efforts ineffectual to raise the Ladder,
they

[30]

they left it upon the Ground, and went again to the Well-side to listen, and hearing the poor Man still groaning, they were a little at a Stand what they should do to put a quick End to the Life of the miserable Creature. But soon recollecting themselves, they hunted about for something heavy to throw in upon him, and found two large Logs of Wood, that had been Gate-Posts, which they threw into the Well; and being resolv'd to do the Business effectually, got together as many great Stones as they could find, and threw them in likewise. And now they thought they had done his Business, and they were undoubtedly right in their Guess, for upon listening again, they could hear nothing of him; and therefore concluding he was quite dead, as most certainly he was, they mounted their Horses, and went to their respective Houses.

Thus are we brought to the fatal and final Catastrophe of the unhappy Chater, and whoever seriously reflects on the Cause for which he suffered, the exquisite Torments he underwent, the Variety of Punishments with which he was continually exercised, from the Time he set out from Rowland's Castle, till he finished his Miseries in Harris's Well, which was from Sunday in the Afternoon, to the Dead of the Night between the Wednesday and Thursday following, must feel their Heart melt with Compassion, and, in some Measure, be sensible of the variegated Pains and Tortures

tures with which the poor Creature was constantly rack'd and torn during this Time. But who can think on the vile Miscreant, his Tormentors, without Horror and Detestation? Bloody Villains! Had you thought that his Death was absolutely necessary, to secure your own Lives, could you not have dispatch'd him at once, without exercising such a Variety of merciless Cruelties upon him? 'Tis true, even in this Case you would not have been excused, because you would have slain him while he was actually discharging his Duty to his Country, that is, in endeavouring to detect, and to bring to condign Punishment, Wretches that live only by Rapine, and the Plunder of the Publick: I say, had this been the Case, and upon meeting him on the Road, you had shot him through the Head with a Pistol, merely to prevent his bringing you to that righteous Judgment which your Country has sinc'd pass'd upon you, it might have been some Mitigation of your Crime: But to torture and destroy a Man by Inches, to be constantly afflicting and lacerating his Body for so many Days together with every Cruelty that Malice itself could suggest; this surely must convince Mankind, that some malicious Demon had taken Possession of your Souls, and banish'd every Sentiment of Humanity from your harden'd Hearts,

But let us now proceed to those other Matters which we promis'd to give an Account of

[32]

of. The first Thing we shall mention, ought indeed to have been taken Notice of before, but were not willing to interrupt the Story of Chater, till we had brought him to the last Stage of his Sufferings, and his dinal Destruction in this World.

When these Miscreants had brought their unhappy Victim within about two Hundred Yards of the Well, Jackson and Carter staid behind, & bid Tapner, Cobby, Stringer, Steel, Perryer, and Hammond go forward, and do their Business: *You,* says Jackson, *go, and do your Duty, and kill* Chater, *as we have done ours in killing* Galley, *and then there will be a final End of the two informing Rogues*; for Hammond, Stringer, Cobby, Tapner, and Perryer, were neither of them concern'd in the Murder of Galley, who was kill'd on Sunday Night, or early on Monday Morning, as before mentioned, of which they were intirely ignorant, till inform'd by Jackson, Carter, Little Harry, Richards, Steel, and Little Sam.

But though these Wretches had perpetrated the Murders of the two unhappy Men, Galley and Chater, with such Secresy, (notwithstanding they had them so long in Hand) that they thought it next to impossible that they should ever be discover'd, unless they had Traitors among themselves; yet they were sensible, that there were two Witnesses still living, which, though dumb, would certainly render them suspected, if suffer'd to survive

heir

their Masters; and these were the two Horses that belong'd to Galley and Chater; and therefore a Consultation was held among them, what was best to be done with them. Some were for turning 'em a-drift in a large Wood, where they might range about a long while before they could be own'd, But others alledg'd that whenever they were found, they would undoubtedly soon be known to belong to their rightful Owners, and as Galley and Chater might possibly have been seen riding upon 'em in their Company, but a very little before those Men were missing, some over-curious People might imagine they were, some way or other, concern'd in conveying them away; to prevent which, let us, said they, carry them to the Sea-side, and put 'em on board the first French Vessel that shall bring Goods on the Coast, and so send 'em to France. This however, was objected to, as liable to some Miscarriage; and therefore, after much Debate, it was unanimously agreed to knock 'em on the Head at once, and then take their Skins off. Accordingly they kill'd the Horse which Galley rode on, which was a Grey, and having flea'd him, cut his Hide into small Bits, which they dispos'd of in such a Manner, that it was impossible for any Discovery to be made from thence. As to the Horse which Chater rode on, which was a Bay, when they came to look for him, in order to serve him in the same manner, they could not find him for he had

F   got

got away, and not long after was deliver'd to his right Owner; but the Grey, which Mr. Shearer, of the Custom-house at Southampton, had hir'd for Mr. Galley, and which they had now kill'd, he was oblig'd to pay for.

Thus we have given a full and circumstantial Account of all the Particulars relating to the Murders of these two unhappy Men, whose Misfortune it was to fall into the Hands of these Savage Brutes. But as Providence seldom suffers such atrocious Crimes to go undiscover'd or unpunish'd even in this World, so in this Case, though the Divine Justice seemed dormant for a while, yet, as we shall presently see, the Eye of Providence was not asleep, but was still watching their Motions, and taking the necessary Steps to bring to Light these horrible Deeds of Darkness, and to punish the villainous Perpetrators of such abominable Wickedness in the most exemplary Manner.

The first Thing that gave Occasion to suspect, that some such Misfortune as above related, had befel these Men, was, that they did not return in the Time which it was reasonable to suppose they might have done, from Major Battin's, to whom Mr. Shearer had sent them with a Letter, as before related. Another Circumstance that served to strengthen the Suspicion, that they had fell into the Hands of Smugglers, who had privately made away with or destroyed them, was, that exactly at
the

[35]
the Time when they were sent on the above-said Message, the Great Coat of Mr. Galley was found on the Road very bloody. This Circumstance the Reader will remember we mention'd when we gave an Account of their first setting out from Rowland's Castle, when these Tormentors began their cruel Discipline of Whipping, and that they pull'd off Galley's Great Coat, that he might the more sensibly feel their Lashes.

The long Absence of these Men from their Homes, and the Reasons there were to conclude that the Smugglers had either murder'd them or sent 'em to France, being laid before the Commissioners of the Customs, and by them before his Majesty in Council, a Proclamation was immediately ordered, offering a Reward to any one who should discover what was become of them, with his Majesty's Pardon to such Discoverer. However, six or seven Months passed before the Government could get the least Light into the Affair; and then a full Discovery was gradually made by the following Means.

One of the Persons who had been a Witness to some of the Transactions of this bloody Tragedy, and knew of the Death of either Galley or Chater, and where one was buried, tho' he was no Way concern'd in the Murder, sent an anonymous Letter to a Person of Distinction, wherein he intimated, that he thought that the Body of one of the Unfortunate Men
that

that were missing, and mention'd in his Majesty's Proclamation, was bury'd in the Sands in a certain Place near Rake ; (but for some particular Reason did not think it prudent to make himself known) whereupon some People went in Search, where they found the Corpse of Galley buried ; and the Reason why it is suppos'd he was bury'd alive, as is before mention'd, they found him standing almost upright, with his Hands covering his Eyes.

This Discovery being made by this Letter, another Letter was sent, wherein an Account was given, that one William Steele, otherwise Hardware, was one concern'd in the Murder of the Man that was found buried in the Sands, and Mention was made therein where they might find him, and he was accordingly taken into Custody ; when he offer'd himself to be an Evidence for the King, and to make a full Discovery and Disclosure of the whole wicked Transaction, and of all the Persons concern'd therein.

Steele being now in Custody, he gave an Acount of the Murder of Galley, and further inform'd in what Manner Chater was murder'd, and thrown into Harris's Well in Lady-Holt Park ; wither Messengers being likewise sent, and one of them let down into the Well, the Body was found with a Rope about his Neck, his Eyes appear'd to have been cut or pick'd out of his Head, and his Boots and Spurs on. They got his Body out of the Well with only
one

[37]

one Leg on, the other was brought up by itself, with the Boot and Spur upon it; which it is suppos'd, was occasion'd by his Fall down the Well, or else by throwing the Logs of Wood and Stones upon him, as has been before related.

But Steele did not only give Information of all the Particulars of this transcendant Wickedness, but he likewise acquainted the Justice with the Names of the principal Actors in it, as I have just before related. Pursuant to which, Warrants were immediately issued, and several of them taken in a short Time, and committed to Gaol.

John Race, who was another of the King's Witnesses, and concern'd with them in the Beinning of the Affair at Rowland's Castle, came in, and voluntarily surrender'd himself, and was admitted an Evidence, as Steele had been.

Hammond was taken the Beginning of October, and being carried before Sir John Miller, and Sir Hutchins Williams, Barts., and it appearing, by undeniable Evidence, that he was privy to, and concern'd in the Murder of Daniel Chater, and throwing him into a Well near Harting, in the County of Sussex, was committed to Horsham Gaol, October the 10th.

John Cobby being likewise apprehended, and carried before the same Gentlemen, was by them committed to Horsham Gaol, the 18th of the same Month, and for the same Crime of murdering Chater.

Benjamin

n Tapner was also committed to the ol the 16th of November following, by the same Gentlemen, and on his own Confession, of murdering Chater in the manner above related. He was betray'd by his Master, one T——ff, a Shoemaker in Chichester of whom we shall have Occasion to speak more at large when we come to give an Account of the Life of Tapner.

Richard Mills jun. was apprehended in Sussex, with George Spencer, Richard Payne, and Thomas Reoff, about the 16th August 1748; and being all brought together, under a strong Guard, to Southwark, were carried before Justice Hammond, who committed them all to the County Gaol for Surry, for being concern'd with divers other Persons ; arm'd with Fire Arms, in running uncustomed Goods, and for not surrendering themselves after Publication in the London Gazette.

And on the 5th Day of October last, Richard Mills was detain'd in the said Gaol, by Virtue of a Warrant under the Hand and Seal of Justice Hammond, for being concerned in the Murder of William Galley & Daniel Chater, whose Bodies had a little before been found, as has been related.

William Jackson and William Carter were taken November the 14th, near Godalming in Surry, and brought up to London, under a strong Guard, the 17th November, and being carried before Justice Poulson in Covent-Garden

Garden, were, after Examination, committed to Newgate, for being concern'd with diverse other Persons, in running uncustomed Goods, and for not surendering after Publication in the London Gazette.

Old Richard Mills, notwithstanding he knew that all these were taken, and that Warrants were out against Henry Sheerman, otherwise Little Harry, of Lye, near Warblington, Labourer; Edmund Richards, of Long-Coppice, in the Parish of Warblington, Labourer; Thomas Stringer of Chichester, Cordwainer; Daniel Perryer, otherwise Little Daniel, of Norton, Labourer; and John Mills (his other Son) of Trotton, Labourer, all which Places are in the County of Sussex; as also against Thomas Willis, commonly called the Coachman of Selbourne, near Liphook; and Samuel Howard, oherwise Little Sam, of Rowland's Castle, Labourer, both in the County of Hants, for being concern'd with the others before mentioned, in the Murders of Galley and Chater, yet he continued at Home, never absconding, thinking himself quite safe, as he knew nothing of the Murder of Galley, and as to that of Chater, he was seemingly very easy, as he was not murder'd in his House, nor he present when the wicked Deed was done: But Steele having given an Account in his Information of the whole Affair, which was laid before the Attorney General, that old Major Mills was concern'd, as has been before related,

[40]

keeping the poor Man chain'd in his
r Turf-house; and that he was pre-
 when they all came down from Scardefield's, and told him they were come to take
Chater up to Harris's Well, where they design'd to murder him, and fling him into it;
as likewise, that he was present in the Turf-
house when Tapner cut Chater across the Eyes,
Nose, and Forehead; and that he did express
the Words, *Don't murder him here; take him
somewhere else, and do it*, it was thought necessary to apprehend him, and accordingly on
the 16th of December last he was taken; and
being brought the next Day before Sir Hutchins Williams and Sir John Miller, they committed him to Horsham Gaol, as being accessary to the Murder of Daniel Chater before
the same was committed, and concealing the
same; which Offence subjects the Person so
guilty to be hang'd.

William Combleach the Gardener, who lent
them the Ladder and Rope to get Chater out
of the Well, when they head him groan, and
found he was not quite dead, having being
heard to say, that some of the Persons in Custody for the Murders had told him they had
murder'd two Informers against the Smugglers, it was thought proper to take him up,
and examine him, in Expectation that some
further Discoveries might be made in this tragical Affair; but when Combleach was brought
before the Magistrates, he refus'd to give satisfactory

tisfactory Answers to the proper Questions as were ask'd him, and very idly and obstinately deny'd all that was sworn against him, whereupon he was committed to Horsham Gaol on Suspicion of being concern'd in the Murder of Daniel Chater.

The Smugglers had reign'd a long Time uncontroul'd ; — the common Officers of the Customs were too few and too weak to encounter them ; they rode in Troops to the Sea-side to fetch their Goods, and carried 'em off in Triumph by Day-light ; nay, so audacious were they grown at last, that they were not afraid of regular Troops, that were sent into the Country to keep them in Awe ; of which we had several Instances. If any one of them happen'd to be taken, and the Proof ever so clear against him, no Magistrate in the Country durst commit him to Gaol ; if he did, he was sure to have his House or Barns set on Fire, or some other terrible Mischief done him, if he was so happy to escape with his Life, which has been the Occasion of their being brought to London to be committed. But for a Man to inform against them, the most cruel and miserable Death was his undoubted Portion ; of which we already have given two melancholy Instances, and could produce more; one especially is so very notorious, that we shall make a little Digression, and relate a few Particulars of it, and reserve a more circumstantial Account till the Trials of these cruel

Villains

Villains are over, who were the horrid Perpetrators of it.

Richard Hawkins, of Yapton, in the County of Sussex, Labourer, being at work in a Barn, two of their Gang, in January 1747-8, came to the Barn in the said Parish of Yapton, where the poor Man was threshing Corn.

The Names of the two Men who came to him, were Jeremiah Curtis, of Hawkhurst in Kent, Butcher, and John Mills, of Trotton in Sussex, Labourer (this last one of those who were concern'd in the Murder of Chater, whose dismal Story we have before related, and who is not yet taken) and having found Hawkins at work, as before mention'd they told him, that he must along with them ; and on his shewing some Reluctance to comply with their Commands, they swore they would shoot him through the Head that Instant if he did not immediately come away without any more Words. Poor Hawkins being terrified at their Threats, put on his Cloaths, and went along with them to the Sign of the Dog & Partridge, an Alehouse on Slindon Common, and going in to a back Room, he saw Thomas Winter, of Posling, near Chichester, and one call'd Rob, or Little Fat Back, Servant to Jeremiah Curtis, who liv'd at or near East-Grinstead, and is Brother to one there who goes by the Name of Cackler. In the back Room of this Alehouse, these two were waiting for them. This was in the Afternoon, and having kept Hawkins

kins there till about twelve o'Clock at Night, took him away; but whither they carried, or what they did with him, was not known for a long Time; for the Man was not seen, nor heard of, till the Body was found in a Pond in Parham Park, belonging to Sir Cecil Bishop, in Sussex, upwards of Nine Months afterwards; and the Coroner's Inquest having sat on the Body, they brought in their Verdict, Wilful Murder, by Persons unknown.

The only Reason these Villains had to commit this Murder on the poor Wretch, who left behind a Wife and many Children, was, on a Supposition only, that he had conceal'd a small Bag of Tea from them; for they had lodg'd a Quantity of run Tea near the Barn where the Man work'd, and when they came to look for it, miss'd one Bag, and imagin'd he had taken it away; tho' the Villains, on a second Search, after they had murder'd the Man, found the Bag of Tea where they had hid it, and had over-look'd it before.

This Murder in itself was as barbarous as that of Mr. Galley's; for they made him go with them upwards of Ten Miles, all the Way whipping him, and beating him with the Handles of their Whips till they had kill'd him; and then tied Stones to his Legs and Arms, and flung him into the Pond, which kept the Body under Water.

These terrible Executions, committed by the Smugglers on these poor Men, and the

dreadful

dreadful Menaces which they utter'd against any Person that should presume to interrupt them in their contraband Trade, so terrified the People every where, that scarce any Body durst look at them as they pass'd through Towns and Villages in large Bodies in open Day-light. And the Custom Officers were so intimated, that hardly any of them had Courage enough to go upon their Duty. Some of them they knew they had already sent to France, others had been kill'd or wounded in opposing them, and that their Brother Galley, in particular, had been inhumanly murder'd by them : So that not only the honest Trader suffer'd by the running of prodigious Quantities of Goods, which were sold again at a Rate which he could not buy them at, unless he traded with them ; but the King's Revenue was considerably lessen'd by this smuggling Traffick.

It is no Wonder, indeed, that when once a Set of Men commenced Smugglers, that they should go on to commit the vilest Excesses ; for when a Man has wrought himself into a firm Persuasion, that it is no Crime to rob his King, or his Country, the Transition is easy to the Belief, that it is no Sin to plunder, or destroy his Neighbour ; and therefore we need not be much surpriz'd, that so many of the Smugglers have turn'd Highwaymen, House-breakers, and Incendiaries, of which we have had but too many Instances of late.

The

The Body of Smugglers was now increas'd to a prodigious Number, and the Mischiefs they did wherever they came, at least whereever they met with Opposition, were so enormous, that the whole Country were afraid of them; and even the Government itself began to be alarm'd, and to apprehend Consequences that might be fatal to the publick Peace, in Case a speedy Check was not put to their audacious Proceedings. His Majesty therefore being perfectly inform'd of their notorious Villainies, and Informations being given of many of the Names of the most desperate of their Gangs, particulary those who broke open the Custom-house Warehouse at Pool, issued out a Proclamation, with Lists of their several Names, declaring, that unless they surrender'd themselves to Justice at a Day appointed, they should be outlaw'd, and out of the Protection of the Laws of their Country; promising a Reward of 500 l. to be paid by the Commissioners of the Customs, for the Apprehension of every one who should be taken, and convicted in Pursuance thereof.

This, in great Measure, has had the desir'd Effect, and several of them have been apprehended, tried, convicted, and executed, which was the only Satisfaction they could make to publick Justice. Many more of them are now in some of his Majesty's Gaols, in order to receive the just Reward of their Crimes; so that the Knot of them seems to be near broke; and

and 'tis to be hoped, that the prudent Measures that have and shall be taken to suppress and keep them under, will prove effectual; at least, that they will never be able to get to such an enormous Height as they have been. But to return from this Digression.

Seven of the notorious Villains, who had confederated in the Murder of Galley and Chater, being apprehended by the Diligence and Assiduity of the Government, the Noblemen and Gentlemen of the County of Sussex, being desirous of making publick Examples of such horrible Offenders, and to tertify others from committing the same, or the like flagitious Crime, requested his Majesty to grant a special Commission to some of his Judges, to hold an Assize on Purpose to try them; and represented, that as Chichester was a City large enough, commodiously to entertain the Judges, and all their Train; and as it was likewise contiguous to the Places where the Murders were committed, they judg'd it the properest Place for the Assizes to be held. Accordingly a Commission pass'd the Seals, to hold a special Assizes there the 16th Day of January, 1748-9.

On Monday the 9th of January, 1748-9, Jackson and Carter were remov'd from Newgate, as also Richard Mills, jun. from the New Goal in Surry, under a strong Guard, to Horsham, in their Way to Chichester. When they came to Horsham, the other five Prisoners, viz. Richard

Richard Mills, sen. Benjamin Tapner, John Hammond, John Cobby, & Wm. Combleach, (committed only on Suspicion) who were already in that Gaol, were all put in a Waggon, and convey'd from thence, under the same Guard as brought the others from London to Chichester, where they arriv'd Friday the 13th.

On their Arrival there, they were all confin'd, being well secur'd with heavy Irons, in one Room, except Jackson, who being extremely ill, was put in a Room by himself, and all imaginable Care was taken of him, in order to keep him alive (for he was in a very dangerous Condition) till he had taken his trial.

Having thus brought the Prisoners to Chichester, and put them in safe Confinement, we shall leave them there for the present, till we meet them again on their Trials, of which we are enabled to give the most authentick Account of any that has been, or may be publish'd. After that, we shall attend the Prisoners while under Sentence of Condemnation, and truly relate whatever appear'd remarkable in their Carriage and Demeanour ; and then bear them Company to the Place of Execution, where we shall take particular Notice of their Behaviour and Dying Words.

But, previous to this, it will be necessary to give some Account of the Journey of the Judges from London to Chichester, in order to rectify

tify some Mistakes that were publish'd of it in the publick Prints.

The Judges set out from London, Friday February the 13th and arriv'd at the Duke of Richmond's House, at Godalming in Surry, that Evening, were they lay that Night, and the next Day set out for Chichester, and where met at Midhurst by his Grace the Duke of Richmond, who entertain'd their Lordships with a Dinner at his Hunting House near Charlton. After they had regal'd themselves a convenient Time, they proceeded on their Journey, and got into Chichester about Five o'Clock, and went directly to the Bishop's Palace. It was reported, tho' very erroneously, that they were guarded in their Journey by a Party of Horse, both thither and back again; but they had none but their own Attendants, except a few Servants of his Grace the Duke of Richmond's in all, about sixty Horsemen; the Judges, Counsellors, and principal Officers being in six Coaches, each drawn by six Horses.

On Sunday Morning, the 15th of January, they went to the Cathedral, accompanied by his Grace the Duke of Richmond, (who is one of the Aldermen of that City) and the Mayor, with the rest of the Aldermen of the Corporation, where an excellent Sermon was preach'd suitable to the solemn Occasion, by the Reverend Mr. ASHBURNHAM, Dean of Chichester.

We shall now proceed to give an Account of what pass'd at Chichester during their Trials;
only

only observe, first, that William Combleach the Gardener (whom we have before observe'd to have been committed only on a Suspicion, by his own idle Talk, which, no doubt, gave a just Foundation for his said Commitment) was not order'd to be indicted, nor from the Mouths of the Witnesses on the Trials his Name was but barely mention'd.

Chichester, January 16th, 1748-9.

THIS Morning, between Eleven and Twelve o'Clock, the Judges assigned to hold the Assizes by Special Commission, viz. the Honourable Sir Michael Foster, Knt. one of the Judges of his Majesty's Court of King's Bench; the Honourable Edward Clive, Esq; one of the Barons of his Majesty's Court of Exchequer; and the Honourable Sir Tho. Birch, Knt. one of the Judges of his Majesty's Court of Common Pleas, went from the Bishop's Palace, preceded by the High Sheriff of the County, with the usual Ceremonies, to the Guildhall, where they were met by his Grace the Duke of Richmond, Sir Richard Mill, Sir Cecil Bishop, Sir Hutchins Williams, Barts. John Butler, Esq; Robert Bull, Esq; and others of the Commissioners named in the Commission for that Purpose; and after having opened the said Commission, and the same being read, the Gentlemen, who were summon'd to be of the Grand Jury, were call'd over, and the following

following Twenty-seven, who were present, sworn, viz.

    Sir John Miller, Bart. Foreman,
    Sir Matthew Featherstonhaugh, Bart.
    Sir Thomas Ridge, Knt.
    John Page, Esq;
    George Bramston, Esq;
    William Battine, Esq;
    John Winker, Esq;
    Edward Tredcroft, Esq;
    William Winker, Esq;
    Samuel Blunt, Esq;
    William Pool, Esq;
    Peckham Williams, Esq;
    Thomas Bettesworth Bilson, Esq;
    Thomas Phipps, Esq;
    William Mitford, Esq;
    James Goble, Esq;
    John Cheal, Esq;
    William Leeves, Esq;
    Richard Nash, Esq;
    Thomas Fowler, Esq;
    William Peckham, Esq;
    William Bartlet, Esq;
    John Hollest, Esq;
    Francis Peachey, Gent.
    John Laker, Gent.
    William Peachey, Gent.
    John Pay, Gent.

So soon as they were sworn, Mr. Justice Foster gave a most learned and judicious Charge,

[51]

Charge, taking Notice, among other Things,
' That this Commission, tho it did not extend
' to all the Crimes which are cognizable un-
' der the General Commissions which are exe-
' cuted in the common Circuits twice each
' Year; yet it did not differ from other Com-
' missions granted for holding the Assizes, so
' that they must proceed on this Commission
' in the same Method of Trial, and the same
' Rules of Evidence as was usually done in
' Commissions of Assizes; That this Commis-
' sion was only to inquire of Murders, Man-
' slaughters, and Felonies committed in the
' County of Sussex, and the Accessaries there-
' to, and therefore the Grand Jury could not
' take Notice of any Thing else, but what was
' specified in the said Commission.

' Then his Lordship was pleas'd to say,
' that the several Murders, and other Crimes,
' committed by armed Persons gather'd toge-
' ther contrary to all Law, in this and the
' neighbouring Counties, loudly demanded
' the Justice of the Nation; and for that Rea-
' son his Majesty, out of his Royal Desire in
' doing Justice, and of his paternal Love for
' his Subjects in these Parts, that their Persons
' might go in Safety, had been pleas'd to en-
' trust his Lordship and Brethren, with his
' special Commission, that publick Justice
' might be done upon the Offenders against
' the publick Laws of this Kingdom, and
' that

'that the Innocent might be releas'd from
'their Confinement.

'His Lordship likewise took Notice, in
'the beginning Part of his Charge, of the
'dangerous Confederacies that had been form-
'ed, for too many Years past, in the County
'of Sussex, and its neighbouring Counties, for
'very unwarrantable, and very wicked Pur-
'poses ; even for robbing the Publick of that
'Revenue which is absolutely necessary to its
'Support, and for defeating the fair Trader in
'his just Expectations of Profit ; and which,
'without mentioning more, are the necessary
'unavoidable Consequences of that Practice
'which now goes under the Name of Smug-
'gling ; and this, his Lordship said, was not
'all, for this wicked Practice had been sup-
'ported by an armed Force ; by Numbers of
'dissolute People assembled together, and
'acting, in open Day-light, in Defiance of all
'the Law, and all the Justice of their Coun-
'try, to the Terror of his Majesty's peaceable
'Subjects ; and had gone so far, in some late
'Instances, as deliberate Murders, attended
'with Circumstances of great Aggravation,
'in Consequence, as it was to be fear'd, of
'those unlawful Combinations.

'His Lordship likewise said, that in Case
'of a Murder, wherever it appear'd that the
'Fact was committed with any Degree of De-
'liberation, and especially where attended with
'Cir-

' Circumstances of Cruelty, the usual Di-
' stinction between Murder and Manslaughter
' could never take Place ; for the Fact is, in
' the Eye of the Law, Wilful Murder, of
' Malice Prepense : And involves every Per-
' son concern'd, as well those aiding and a-
' betting, as those who actually commit the
' Fact, in the same Degree of Guilt.

' His Lordship was pleas'd further to take
' Notice, that where a Number of People en-
' gage together with a felonious Design, ei-
' ther for Murder, Robbery, or any other Fe-
' lony, every Person so engag'd, and present
' aiding and abetting in the Fact, is consider'd
' as a Principal in the Felony : And the Rea-
' son the Laws goes upon, is this, that the
' Presence of every one of the Accomplices
' gives Countenance, Encouragement, and Se-
' curity to all the rest ; so that consequently
' the Fact is consider'd, in the Eye of the
' Law, and of sound Reason too, as the Act
' of the whole Party, tho' it be perpetrated
' by the Hands only of one ; for he is consi-
' der'd as the Instrument by which the others
' act.

[*As the Remainder of his Lordship's Charge tends for the Good of the Publick ; and particularly very necessary for most Persons to read, that they may know how far they are acting contrary to the Law, and by this Knowledge it may prevent many from running Headlong into any of these violent*

violent and villainous Practices, we think we cannot do better than to relate the same.]

' And when we say, continued his Lord-
' ship, that the Presence of a Person at the
' Commission of a Felony will involve him
' in the Guilt of the rest, we must not confine
' ourselves to a strict, actual Presence, such a
' Presence as would make him an Eye or Ear
' Witness of what passes. For an Accomplice
' may be involv'd in the Guilt of the rest, tho'
' he may happen to be so far distant from the
' Scene of Action, as to be utterly out of sight
' or hearing of what passes.
' For Instance ; If several Persons agree to
' commit a Murder, or other Felony, and
' each Man takes his Part : Some are appoint-
' ed to commit the Fact, others to watch at
' a Distance, to present a Surprize, or to fa-
' vour the Escape of those who are more im-
' mediately engag'd ; the Law says, that if
' the Felony be committed, it is the Act of all
' of them : For each Man operated in his Sta-
' tion towards the Commission of it, at one
' and the same Instant. And so much doth
' the Law abhor Combinations of this Kind,
' especially where innocent Blood is shed, that
' a Man may, in Judgment of Law, be in-
' volv'd in the Guilt of Murder, when possi-
' bly his Heart abhorr'd the Thoughts of it.
' For if Numbers of People assemble in Pro-
' secution of any unlawful Design, with a Re-
' solution

' solution to stand by each other against all
' Opposers, and a Murder is committed by
' one of the Party in Prosecution of that De-
' sign, every Man so engaged at the Time of
' the Murder, is in the Eye of the Law equally
' guilty with him that gave the Stroke.

' Many Cases might be put which come un-
' der this Rule. I will confine myself to a
' few which the present Solemnity naturally
' suggests.

' For Instance; Numbers of People assemble
' for the Purpose of running uncustomed
' Goods, or for any of the Purposes which
' now go under the general Term of Smug-
' gling, with a Resolution to resist all Oppo-
' sers; (and the riding with Fire-Arms and
' other offensive Weapons is certainly an Evi-
' dence of that Resolution) Numbers of Peo-
' ple, I say, assemble in this Manner, and for
' this Purpose. They are met by the Officers
' of the Revenue: One of the Party, *in Pro-*
' *secution of this unlawful Design,* fires on the
' King's Officer, and kills him or any of his
' Assistants: The whole Party is, in the Eye
' of the Law, guilty of Murder, though their
' original Intention went no farther than Smug-
' ling. For that Intention being unlawful,
' the killing in Prosecution of that Intent is
' Murder. And every Man engaged in it,
' partakes of the Guilt. The Act of one, in
' Prosecution of their common Engagement, is
' consider'd as the Act of all.

' I

' I will go one Step further; the Party assembled in the Manner and for the Purposes I have mention'd is met by the King's Officers, and an Affray happens between them. During the Affray one of the Party fires at the King's Officers, but misses his Aim and kills one of his own Party, perhaps his nearest Relation or Bosom Friend (if People of that Character are capable of true Friendship) this is Murder in him, and in the whole Party too. For if a Man upon Malice against another strikes at him, and by Accident kills a third Person, the Law, as it were, transfers the Circumstance of Malice from him that was aimed at, to him that received the Blow and died by it. And consequently, in the Case I have just put, the Person who discharged the Gun being guilty of Murder, all his Accomplices are involved in his Guilt; because the Gun was discharged in Prosecution of their common Engagement, and it is therefore consider'd as the Act of the whole Party.

' What I have hitherto said regards those who are present in the Sense I have mentioned, and abetting the Fact at the Time of the Commission of it. But there are others who may be involved in the same Guilt, I mean the Accessaries before the Fact. These are all People who by Advice, Persuasion, or any other Means, procure the Fact to be done, but cannot be said, in any Sense,

' to

[57]

' to be present at the actual Perpetration of it.

' These Persons are involved in the Guilt,
' and liable in the Case of wilful Murder, to
' the same Punishment as the principal Of-
' fenders are.

' I am very sensible, Gentlemen, that I
' have been something longer than I needed to
' have been, if I had spoken barely for your
' Information. But in this Place, and upon
' this Occasion, I thought it not improper to
' enlarge on some Points, that People may
' see, and consider in Time, the infinite Ha-
' zard they run by engaging in the wicked
' Combinations I have mentioned ; and how
' suddenly and fatally they may, being so en-
' gaged, be involved in the Guilt of Murder
' itself, while perhaps their principal View
' might fall very short of that Crime.

His Lordship having ended his Charge, two Bills of Indictment were presented to the Grand Jury, one for the Murder of William Galley sen. a Custom-house Officer in the Port of Southampton, and the other for the Murder of Daniel Chater, of Fordingbridge in the County of Hants, Shoemaker ; when, as soon as the Grand Jury had receiv'd the Bills, they withdrew to the Council Chamber in the North-Street ; and the following Persons were sworn to give Evidence before them, who immediately after their being severally sworn in Court, went and attended the Grand Jury ; viz. William Steel, alias Hardware, and John Race, o-
I therwise

[58]

otherwise Raise, (two Accomplices in the said Murders) Mr. Milner, Collector of the Customs at the Port of Poole ; Mr. Shearer, Collector of the Customs at the Port of Southampton ; William Galley, Son of the Deceased William Galley ; Edward Holton, George Austin, Tho. Austin, Robert Jenkes, Joseph Southern, William Garrat, William Lamb, Richard Kent, Ann Pescod, William Scardefield, Edward Soanes, Mrs. Chater, the Widow of the deceased William Chater, John Greentree, George Poate, and Mr. Brackstone. And then the Court adjourn'd till Nine o'Clock the next Morning.

P. S. Before we go on any further, we think it proper to inform the Readers, that we shall now proceed to the several Circumstances attending the Trials of the seven bloody Wretches ; and tho' it may be almost a Repetition of what has already been related, yet there are many Facts which we have not as yet taken Notice of, and without which Account of the Trials this Work would not be compleat ; which when done, we shall proceed with the Lives, &c. of these Miscreants as before promised.

Chichester, January 18, 1748-9

THE Judges went to the Court this Morning about Nine o'Clock, where his Grace the Duke of Richmond had been
some

[59]

some Time; and the Court being sat, the seven following Prisoners, viz. Benjamin Tapner, John Cobby, John Hammond, *Wm. Jackson, William Carter, Richard Mills the younger and Richard Mills the elder, (who were all brought under a strong Guard from the Gaol,) were put to the Bar, the Grand Jury having return'd both the Bills found into Court, and arraigned upon the Indictment for the Murder of Daniel Chater; the three first as Principals, and the other four as Accessaries before the Fact.

The Clerk of the Arraigns calling upon the several Prisoners at the Bar to hold up their Hands, which being done, he read the Indictment aloud, which was as follows, viz.

That you Benjamin Tapner, John Cobby, and John Hammond, together with Thomas Stringer and Daniel Perryer, not yet taken, not having the Fear of God before your Eyes, but being moved and seduced by the Instigation of the Devil, upon the 19th Day of February, in the 21st Year of his present Majesty's Reign, with Force of Arms at the Parish of Harting, in the County of Sussex, in and upon one Daniel Chater, being then and there in the Peace of God, and his said Majesty, feloniously, wilfully, and out of your Malice aforethought, did make an Assault; and that you the said

Benjamin

---

* Jackson was so ill he was obliged to be brought in a Chair; and likewise was permitted to have a Chair, and sat during the Time of both his Trials.

Benjamin Tapner, a certain Cord or Rope made of Hemp, of the Value of Sixpence, which you the said Benjamin Tapner had then and there in your Hands, about the Neck of him the said Daniel Chater, then and there with Force of Arms, feloniously, wilfully, and out of your Malice aforethought, did put, bind, and fasten; and that you the said Benjamin Tapner, with the Rope aforesaid by him, about the Neck of the said Chater, so put, bound, and fastened as aforesaid, him the said Chater, then and there with Force and Arms, feloniously, wilfully, and out of your Malice aforethought, did choak and strangle, of which said choaking and strangling of him the said Chater, in Manner aforesaid, he the said Chater did then and there die. And that you the said John Cobby, and John Hammond, together with Thomas Stringer and Daniel Perryer, both not yet taken, at the Time of the Felony and Murder aforesaid, by him the said Benjamin Tapner, so feloniously, wilfully, and out of his Malice aforethought, done perpetrated, and committed, as aforesaid, then and there feloniously, wilfully, and out of your Malice aforethought, were present, aiding, abetting, comforting, and maintaining the said Benjamin Tapner, the said Daniel Chater in Manner and Form aforesaid, feloniously, wilfully, and out of his Malice aforethought, to kill and Murder. And so that you the said Benjamin Tapner, John Cobby,
John

[61]

John Hammond, together with Thomas Stringer and Daniel Perryer, not yet taken, the said Daniel Chater in Manner and Form aforesaid, then and there with Force and Arms, feloniously, wilfully, and out of your Malice aforethought, did kill and murder against his Majesty's Peace, his Crown and Dignity.—And that you Richard Mills the elder, Richard Mills the younger, Wm. Jackson and William Carter, together with John Mills, Thomas Willis, and Edmund Richards, not yet taken, before the Felony and Murder aforesaid, by them the said Benjamin Tapner, John Cobby, John Hammond, Thomas Stringer and Daniel Perryer, in Manner and Form aforesaid, feloniously, wilfully, and out of your Malice aforethought, done, perpetrated, and committed, (to wit) upon the said 19th Day of February, in the 21st Year aforesaid, at the Parish of Harting aforesaid, in the County of Sussex aforesaid, them the said Benjamin Tapner, John Cobby, John Hammond, Thomas Stringer and Daniel Perryer, the Felony and Murder aforesaid, in Manner and Form aforesaid, feloniously, wilfully, maliciously and out of your Malice aforethought, to do, perpetrate, and commit, feloniously, wilfully, and out of your Malice aforethought, did incite, move, instigate, stir up, counsel, persuade, and procure, against his Majesty's Peace, his Crown and Dignity.

To

To which Indictment they severally pleaded Not Guilty.

This being done, William Jackson and William Carter were arraigned upon the other Indictment, as Principals in the Murder of William Gally, otherwise called William Galley.

Which Indictment the Clerk of the Arraigns read aloud to them as follow, That you William Jackson and William Carter (together with Samuel Downer, alias Howard, alias Little Sam, Edmund Richards and Henry Sheerman, alias Little Harry, not yet taken) not having the Fear of God before your Eyes, but being moved and seduced by the Instigation of the Devil, upon the 15th of February in the 21st Year of his present Majesty's Reign, with Force and Arms, at Rowland's Castle in the County of Southampton, in and upon one William Gally, otherwise called William Galley, being then and there in the Peace of God and his said Majesty, feloniously, wilfully, and out of your Malice aforethought, did make an Assault, and him the said William Gally, upon the Back of a certain Horse, then and there with Force and Arms, feloniously, wilfully, and out of your Malice aforethought, did put and set, and the Legs of him the said William Galley, being so put and set upon the Back of the said Horse as aforesaid with a certain Rope or Cord made of Hemp, under the Belly of the said Horse, then and there with Force and Arms, feloniously, wilfully, and out of your Malice

Malice aforethought, did bind, tie, and fasten; and him the said William Galley, being so put and set upon Horseback as aforesaid, with his Legs so bound, tied, and fastened under the Horse's Belly, as aforesaid, with certain large Whips, which you had then and there in your Right Hands, in and upon the Head, Face, Neck, Shoulders, Arms, Back, Belly, Sides, and several other Parts of the Body of him the said William Galley, then and there with Force and Arms, feloniously, wilfully, and out of your Malice aforethought, for the Space of one Mile, did whip, lash, beat, and strike; by Reason whereof, the said William Galley, was then and there very much wounded, bruised, and hurt; and not being able to endure or bear the Misery, Pain and Anguish, occasioned by his having been so whipped, lashed, beat, and struck, as aforesaid; and by his being so wounded, bruised, and hurt, as aforesaid, then and there dropped down the left Side of the said Horse, on which he then and there rode, with his Head under the Horse's Belly, and his Legs and Feet across the Saddle upon the Back of the said Horse, upon which you the said William Jackson, and William Carter, together with Samuel Downer, otherwise Howard, otherwise Little Sam, Edmund Richards, & Henry Sheeman, otherwise Little Harry, not yet taken, then and there untied the Legs of the said Wm. Galley; and him the said Galley, in & upon the same Horse, then and

and there, with Force and Arms, feloniously, wilfully, and out of your Malice aforethought, did again put and set, and the Legs of him the said William Galley being again so put and set upon the said Horse as last aforesaid, with the same Rope or Cord under the Belly of the said Horse, you then and there with Force and Arms, feloniously, wilfully, and out of your Malice aforethought, under the Horse's Belly, did again bind, tie, and fasten; and him the said William Galley* being again so put and set upon the said Horse, as last aforesaid, with his Legs so bound, tied, and fasten'd under the Horse's Belly, as last aforesaid, with the said Whips which you had then and there in your Right Hands, as aforesaid, in and upon the Head, Face, Neck, Arms, Shoulders, Back, Belly, Sides and several other Parts of the Body of him the said William Galley, you then and there with Force and Arms, feloniously, wilfully, and out of your Malice aforethought, for the Space of half a Mile further, did again whip, lash, beat, and strike; by Reason whereof he the said William Galley was then and there much more wounded, bruised, and hurt; and not being able to endure or bear the Misery, Pain, and Anguish, occasion'd by his having been so whipped, lashed, beat, and struck, in Manner as aforesaid; and by

* Tho' Chater, as well as Galley, was tied on the same Horse, and in the same Manner with him, yet in the Indictment it only mention'd the Name of William Galley.

[65]

by his being so wounded, bruised, and hurt, in Manner as aforesaid, did then and there drop a second Time from off the said Horse, with his Head under the Horse's Belly, and his Legs and Feet across the Saddle. Upon which you the said William Jackson, and William Carter, together with the said Samuel Downer, otherwise Howard, otherwise Little Sam, Edmund Richards, and Henry Sheeman, otherwise Little Harry, not yet taken, then and there again untied the Legs of him the said William Galley, and him, in and upon another Horse, behind a certain other Person, did then and there with Force and Arms, feloniously, wilfully, and out of your Malice aforethought, put and set, and the said William Galley being so put and set on Horseback, as last aforesaid, with the same Whips which you had then and there in your Right Hands as aforesaid, in and upon the Head, Face, Neck, Arms, Shoulders, Back, Belly, Sides, and several other Parts of the Body of the said William Galley, did then and there with Force and Arms, feloniously, wilfully, and out of your Malice aforethought, for the Space of Two Miles Further, until you came into the Parish of Harting, in the County of Sussex aforesaid, again whip, lash, beat, and strike, by Reason whereof the said William Galley was then and there much more wounded, bruised and hurt ; and not being able to endure or bear the Misery, Pain,

K and

and Anguish, occasioned by his having been so wounded, bruised, and hurt, in manner as aforesaid, then and there in the Parish of Harting aforesaid, got off the said Horse; upon which you the said William Jackson, and William Carter, together with Samuel Downer, otherwise Howard, otherwise Little Sam, Edmund Richards, & Henry Sheeman, otherwise Little Harry, not yet taken, him the said Wm. Galley, in and upon another Horse, whereon the said Edmund Richards then and there rode, with the Belly of him the said William Galley across the Pummel of the Saddle, on which the said Richards then and there rode, then and there with Force and Arms, feloniously, wilfully, and out of your Malice aforethought, did put and lay; but before you had gone the Space of eighty Yards further, William Galley not being able to bear the Motion of the said Horse, on which he was so put and laid as last aforesaid, by Reason of having been so whipped, lashed, beat, and struck as aforesaid; and by Reason of his being so wounded, bruised, and hurt, in manner as aforesaid, then and there tumbled off the said Horse, and fell upon the Ground in the common Highway there, by which Fall he the said Wm. Galley was then and there much more wounded, bruised, and hurt; whereupon you the said William Jackson, Wm. Carter, together with Samuel Downer, otherwise Howard, otherwise Little Sam, Edmund Richards, and Henry Sheerman, otherwise
Little

Little Harry, not yet taken, him the said William Galley, in and upon another Horse by himself, then and there with Force and Arms, feloniously, wilfully, and out of your Malice aforethought, did put and set; but the said William Galley, not being able to sit upright upon the said last mention'd Horse, he the said Henry Sheerman, otherwise Little Harry, did then and there get up upon the same Horse, behind him the said William Galley, in order to hold him on; but after you the said William Jackson and William Carter, together with Samuel Downer, otherwise Howard, otherwise Little Sam, Edmund Richards, and Henry Sheeman, otherwise Little Harry, not yet taken, and the said William Galley, had rode on a Quarter of a Mile further together, in manner aforesaid he the said William Galley, not being able to sit upon the said Horse, or ride any further upon the same through the great Misery, Pain, and Anguish, occasioned by his having been so whipped, lashed, beat, and struck, as aforesaid; and by his being so wounded, bruised, and hurt, in manner as aforesaid, then and there tumbled off the said Horse, on which he was so put and set as last aforesaid, and again fell to the Ground; and as he tumbled and fell, the said Henry Sheerman, otherwise Little Harry, who rode behind the said William Galley, and upon the same Horse with him, in manner aforesaid, then and there with Force and Arms, felo-

niously

niously, wilfully, and out of his Malice aforethought, gave to him the said William Galley a most violent Thrust and Push; by Reason whereof the said William Galley then and there fell, with much more Weight and Force to the Ground, than otherwise he would have done; and was thereby then and there much more wounded, bruised and hurt. And that by Reason, of the said binding, tying, and fastening, of him the said William Galley, by you the said William Jackson, and William Carter, together with Samuel Downer, otherwise Howard, otherwise Little Sam, Edmund Richards, and Henry Sheerman, otherwise Little Harry, not yet taken, in Manner and Form aforesaid; and of the whipping, lashing, beating, and striking, of him the said William Galley, by you, in Manner and Form aforesaid; and of the several Wounds, Bruises, and Hurts, which he the said William Galley received, from such whipping, lashing, beating, and striking, in Manner aforesaid, and other Wounds, Bruises, and Hurts, which he the said William Galley so received from the several Falls which he so had from off the said Horses, on which he was so by you put, set, and laid, in Manner aforesaid; and of the said Thrust and Push, which he the said Henry Sheerman, otherwise Little Harry, so as aforesaid, gave him the said William Galley, as he the said William Galley so tumbled and fell from off the said Horse, as last aforesaid;

[69]

said; he the said William Galley, at the Parish of Harting aforesaid, in the County of Sussex aforesaid, did die. And further, That you the said William Jackson, and William Carter, together with the said Samuel Downer, alias Howard, alias Little Sam, Edmund Richards, and Henry Sheerman, alias Little Harry, not yet taken, him the said William Galley, with Force and Arms in Manner and Form aforesaid, feloniously, wilfully, and out of your Malice aforethought, did Kill, and Murder against his Majesty's Peace, his Crown and Dignity.

The Indictments being both read to them, Mr. Justice Foster, before the Jury was call'd, acquainted the Prisoners they might each of them challenge twenty of the Pannel, without shewing Cause; but if they challeng'd more, they must shew a reasonable Cause for so doing; and that if they agreed to join in their Challenges they might be tried together, but if they did not, they would be tried separately, and left them to act in that Behalf as they should see proper.

The Prisoners then consulted among themselves, for a little while, and then agreed to join and be tried together. And then the Jury were sworn, and charg'd by the Clerk of the Arraignments, whose Names were as follows, viz.

John

[70]

John Burnand, Foreman,
William Faulkner,
Richard North,
William Halsted,
Henry Halsted,
John Woods,
John Hipkins,
William Hobbs,
John Shotter,
Thomas Stuart,
William Poe,
Christopher Wilson.

The Council for the King, were Henry Banks, Esq; Member of Parliament for Corff Castle in Dorsetshire, Sidney Strafford Smythe, Esq; Member of Parliament for East Grinstead in Sussex, and two of his Majesty's Council learned in the Law; also Mr. Burrel, Mr. Purkes, and Mr. Steel, Recorder of Chichester.

Mr. Steele open'd the Indictment, as soon as the Jury were sworn, against the Prisoners; after which Mr. Banks very judiciously and learnedly laid down the Facts attending the Murder, which we choose to give our Readers in his own Words;

Council for the King. This is an Indictment against the seven Prisoners at the Bar, for the Murder of Daniel Chater. It is against the three first, viz. Benjamin Tapner, John Cobby, and

and John Hammond, as Principals in that Murder, by being present, aiding, abetting, and assisting therein ; and against Thomas Stringer and Daniel Perryer, as Principals also, and who are not yet apprehended. And it is against the four last Prisoners, viz. William Jackson, William Carter, Richard Mills the younger, as Accessaries before the Murder ; and also against three others as Accessaries before the Fact, viz. John Mills, another Son of Richard Mills the elder, Thomas Willis, and Edmund Richards, not yet taken and brought to Justice.

Although this Indictment hath made a Distinction between the several Prisoners, and divided them into two Classes, of Principals and Accessaries ; yet the Law makes no Distinction in the Crime. And in Case all the Prisoners are guilty of the Charge in this Indictment, they will be all equally liable to the same Judgment and Punishment.

In the Outset of this Trial I shall not enlarge upon the Heinousness of Murder in general ; nor shall I dwell upon those many Circumstances of Aggravation, attending this Murder in particular. When I come to mention those aggravating Circumstances of Cruelty and Barbarity, in the Course of this Trial, I doubt not but they will have all that Effect upon the Gentlemen of the Jury, which they ought to have ; to awaken and fix your Attention to every Part of this bloody Transaction

action; and to balance that Compassion which you feel for the Prisoners, though they felt none for others. The Effect I mean these Circumstances should and ought to have, is, to clear the Way for that Justice which the Nation expects, and calls for from your Determination and Verdict.

To comply with this general Demand of Justice upon the Prisoners, his Majesty (ever attentive to the Good and Welfare of the Kingdom, the Preservation of his Subjects, the Protection of the Innocent, and the Punishment of the Guilty,) in order to give the Prisoners the earliest Opportunity of proving their Innocence, and of wiping off this foul Suspicion of Murder they now lie under, or if guilty of a Breach of the Laws of God and Man, that they may suffer the Punishment due to their Guilt, his Majesty has been pleased, by a Special Commission, to appoint this Trial to be before their Lordships, not less knowing in the Laws, than tender and compassionate in the Execution of them.

I cannot here omit taking Notice of the unhappy Cause of this fatal Effect, now under your Consideration. Every one here present, will in his own Thoughts anticipate my Words ; and knows, I mean Smuggling. Smuggling is not only highly injurious to Trade, a Violation of the Laws, and the Disturber of the Peace and Quiet of all the Maritime Counties in the Kingdom ; but it is a

Nursery

Nursery for all Sorts of Vice and Wickedness; a Temptation to commit Offences at first unthought of; an Encouragement to perpetrate the blackest of Crimes without Provocation or Remorse; and is in general productive of Cruelty, Robbery, and Murder.

It is greatly to be wished, both for the Sake of the Smugglers themselves, and for the Peace of this County, that the dangerous and armed Manner now used of running uncustomed Goods, was less known, and less practised here.

It is a melancholy Consideration to observe, that the best and wisest Measures of Government, calculated to put a Stop to this growing Mischief, have been perverted and abused to the worst of Purposes. And what was intended to be a Cure to this Disorder, has been made the Means to increase and heighten the Disease.

Every Expedient of Lenity and Mercy was at first made use of, to reclaim this abandoned Set of Men. His Majesty, by repeated Proclamations of Pardon, invited them to their Duty and to their own Safety. But instead of laying hold of so gracious an Offer, they have set the Laws at Defiance, have made the Execution of Justice dangerous in the Hands of Magistracy, and have become almost a Terror to Government itself.

The Number of the Prisoners at the Bar, and of others involved in the Suspicion of the same Guilt, the Variety of Circumstances attending this whole Transaction, the Length of Time in the Completion thereof, and the general Expectation of Mankind to be informed of every minute Circumstance leading and tending to finish this Scene of Horror, will necessarily lay me under an Obligation of taking up more Time than will be either agreeable to the Court, or to myself.

To avoid Confusion in stating such a Variety of Facts, with the Evidence and Proofs thereof ; and to fix and guide the Attention of the Gentlemen of the Jury to the several particular Parts of this bloody Tragedy, at last compleated in the Murder of Chater, I shall divide the Facts into four distinct Periods of Time.

1st. What happened precendent to Chater's coming to a Publick House, the Sign of the White Hart, at Rowland's Castle in Hampshire, kept by Elizabeth Paine, Widow, upon Sunday the 14th of February, 1747-8.

And this Period of Time will take in, the Occasion and Grounds of the Prisoners wicked Malice to the Deceased, and the Cause and Motive to his Murder.

2d. What happen'd after Chater's Arrival at the Widow Paine's, to the Time of his being carried away from thence by some of the Prisoners, to the House of Richard Mills the Elder, at Trotton in Sussex.

This will disclose a Scene of Cruelty and Barba-

[75]

Barbarity, previous to Chater's Murder, and shew how active and instrumental the Prisoners Jackson and Carter were therein.

3d. What happen'd after Chater was brought to the House of Richard Mills the Elder, to the Time of his Murder, upon Wednesday Night the 17th of that February.

This will take in the barbarous Usage of Chater at Mills's House; a Consultation of sixteen * Smugglers in what Manner to dispose of Chater, and their unanimous Resolution to murder him; and will shew Tapner, Cobby, and Hammond, to be principals therein, and the other four Prisoners to be Accessaries.

4th, and last Period, takes in the Discovery of Chater's Body in a Well, where he was hung, with the Proofs that it was the Body of Chater.

In the opening of this Case, it will be impossible for me to avoid the frequent mention of one William Galley, also suspected to have been murder'd; and for whose Murder two of the Prisoners, viz. Jackson and Carter, are indicted, and are to be tried upon another Indictment.

But the Murder of Galley is not the Object of your present Consideration, nor do I mention his Name, either to aggravate this Crime, by taking Notice of his Murder also, nor to

inflame

---

* There were sixteen in the whole, with Race and Steel, the two admitted Evidences for the King.

inflame the Jury against the Prisoners at the Bar: But I do it for the Sake of Method, and for the Purpose only of laying the whole Case before the Jury; for the Story of Chater's Murder cannot be told, without disclosing also what happened to Galley, his Companion and Fellow-Sufferer.

To begin with the first Period of Time. Some Time in September 1747, a large Quantity of uncustomed Tea had been duly seized by one Captain Johnson, out of a Smuggling Cutter, and by him lodged in the Custom-House of Poole, in the County of Dorset.

In the Night of the 6th of October following, the Custom-House of Poole was broke open by a numerous and armed Gang of Smugglers; and the Tea which had been seized and there lodged, was by them taken and carried away.

This Body of Smugglers, in their Return from Poole, passed through Fordingbridge in Hants, where Dimer*, one of that Company, was seen and known by Chater. Dimer was afterwards taken up upon Suspicion of being one of those who had broke open the Custom-House of Poole, and was in Custody at Chichester for further Examination, and for

* In the former Part of this Account we call'd his Name Dimer, otherwise Diamond, for he was as frequently call'd by the one as the other; but as he was nam'd by the Council Dimer, so we shall keep to that Name where he was so call'd.

[77]

for further Proof that he was one of that Gang.

And in order to prove the Identity of Dimer, and that he was one of that Gang, Daniel Chater, a Shoemaker at Fordingbridge, (the Person murder'd) was sent in Company with and under the Care of William Galley, a Tidewaiter of Southampton, by Mr. Sheerer, Collector of the Customs there, with a Letter to Major Battine, a Justice of Peace for Sussex, and Surveyor General of the Customs for that County. Sunday Morning the 14th of February, 1747-8, Galley and Chater set out from Southampton, with Mr. Sheerer's Letter, on their Journey to Major Battine's House, at East-Marden, in the Neighbourhood of Chichester.

At the New Inn at Leigh *, in Havant Parish, in Hants, Chater and Galley met with Robert Jenkes, George Austen and Tho. Austen, and having shew'd them the Direction of the Letter to Major Battine, they told them they were going towards Stanstead, where Chater and Galley were informed Major Battine then was; and said they would go with them, and shew them the Road. Their direct Way to Stanstead lay near to Rowland's Castle; but Jenkes and the two Austens carried them to Rowland's Castle that Sunday about Noon, where

* Mr. Bankes omitted here speaking of his calling first on Mr. Holton in the Village of Havant, but that will appear in its proper Place.

where this cruel Plot was first contrived, and in Part carried into Execution.

The Malice conceived by the Prisoners against Chater, from what I have already mentioned, appears not to have arisen from any Injury, or Suspicion of Injury, done by the Deceased to the Prisoners. But because Chater dared to give Information against a Smuggler, and to do his Duty in assisting to bring a notorious and desperate Offender to Justice, he was to be treated with the utmost Cruelty, his Person was to be tortured, and his Life at last destroy'd. What avail the Laws of Society, where no Man dares to carry them into Execution ? Where is the Protection of Liberty and Life, if Criminals assume to themselves a Power of restraining the one, and destroying the other ?

Having mentioned the Motive of the Prisoners to this Murder, I shall now open to you (what I proposed in the second Period of Time) a Scene of Cruelty and Barbarity, tending to the Murder of Chater, begun at Rowland's Castle, by the two Prisoners Jackson and Carter, in Company with others ; and from thence continued, until Chater was brought to the House of Richard Mills the Elder, at Trotton, upon Monday morning the 15th of February before it was Light.

And here you will observe, how cruelly and wickedly, in general, the Gang assembled at Rowland's Castle behaved ; and in particular,

lar, how active Jackson and Carter appear'd in every Step of this fatal Conspiracy.

Soon after Chater and Galley, and the three others, had arrived at Rowland's Castle, the Widow Payne suspected Chater and Galley intended some Mischief against the Smugglers; and for that Purpose inquired of Geo. Austen who the two Strangers were, and what their Business was. He privately inform'd her, they were going to Major Battine with a Letter. She desired, he would either direct the two Strangers to go a different Way from Major Battine's, or would detain them a short Time at her House, until she could send for Jackson, Carter, and others. And she immediately sent her Son William for the Prisoner Jackson; and soon afterwards ordered her other Son Edmund to summon the other Prisoner Carter, and Edmund Richards, Samuel Howard, Henry Sheerman, William Steel, and John Raiss; who all liv'd near Rowland's Castle, and accordingly they all came, as also did Jackson's and Carter's Wives. They were immediately informed by the Widow Paine of what she suspected, and had been informed concerning the two Strangers. Jackson and Carter being very desirous of seeing the Letter to Major Battine, got Chater out of the House, and endeavoured to persuade him to let him see the Letter, and to inform them of the Errand to Major Battine. But upon Galley's coming out to them, and interposing

posing to prevent Chater's making any Discovery, they quarrelled with Galley, and beat him to the Ground : Galley complained of this ill Usage, and said he was the King's Officer, and to convince them shewed his Deputation.

Chater and Galley were very uneasy at this Treatment, and wanted to be gone ; but the Gang insisted upon their staying ; and in order to secure and get them entirely into their own Power, they plied them with strong Liquors, and made them drunk ; and then carried them into another Room to sleep.

During the two Hours Galley and Chater slept, the Letter was taken out of Chater's Pocket ; whereby it appeared that Chater was going to give Information against Dimer. The Secret being thus disclosed to the Gang, the next thing to be considered of by the Smugglers, was how to save their Accomplice Dimer, and to punish Chater and Galley for daring to give Information against him. For that Purpose, whilst Chater and Galley were asleep, several Consultations where held.

It was propos'd first to put Galley and Chater out of the Way, to prevent their giving Information against Dimer ; and to that End it was talk'd of murdering them, and flinging them into a Well, a Quarter of a Mile from Rowland's Castle, that was in the Horse Pasture ; but the Proposal was over-ruled,
fearing,

fearing a Discovery, as the Well was so near Rowland's Castle.

The next Thing proposed was secretly to convey Chater and Galley into France, at that Time at War with England.

The second Scheme was, for all present to contribute three Pence a Week, for the Maintenance of Chater and Galley, who were to be confined in some private Place, and there subsisted until Dimer should be tried; and as Dimer was done unto, so Chater and Galley were to be dealt with.

The third and last Proposal, was to murder both.

With a View and Intention to execute this last, and the most cruel Proposal, Jackson went into the Room about Seven that Evening, where Chater and Galley lay asleep, and awak'd them. They both came out very bloody, and cut in their Faces; but by what means, or what Jackson had there done to them, does not appear. They were immediately afterwards forc'd out of the House by Jackson and Carter; the others present, consenting and assisting; Richards, one of the Company, with a cock'd Pistol in his Hand, swore he would shoot any Person through the Head, who should make the least Discovery of what had passed there.

Chater and Galley were put upon one Horse; and to prevent their Escape, their Legs were tied under the Horse's Belly; and both their

Legs tied together; and the Horse was led by William Steel. After they had been thus carried about one hundred Yards from Rowland's Castle, Jackson cried out to Carter and the Company, *Lick them, Damn them, Cut them, Slash them, Whip them.* Upon which, they whipped and beat them over their Heads, Faces, Shoulders, and other Parts of their Bodies, for the Space of near a Mile. With this cruel Treatment they both fell down under the Horse's Belly, with their Heads dragging upon the Ground. They were again put upon the Horse, and tied as before; and whipp'd and beat with the like Severity, along the Road for upwards of half a Mile. And when they cried out through the Agony of their Pain, Pistols were held to their Heads, and they were threat'ned to be shot, if they made the least Noise or Cry. Being unable to endure this continued and exquisite Pain, and to sit on Horseback any longer, they fell a second Time to the Ground. By this inhuman Usage, they were rendered incapable of supporting themselves any longer on Horseback. Galley was afterwards carried behind Steel, and Chater behind Howard. The Prisoners Jackson and Carter, with the rest of the Company, still continued their merciless Treatment of Chater and Galley; but instead of whipping, they now began to beat them on their Heads and Faces, with the Butt-end of their Whips, loaded with Lead. When they

they came to Lady Holt Park in Sussex, Galley almost expiring with the Torture he had underwent, got down from behind Steel; and it was proposed to throw him alive into a Well adjoining to that Park; in which Well Chater was three Days after hanged by the same Gang. Galley was then thrown across the Pummel of the Saddle, and carried before Richards. He was afterwards laid along alone upon a Horse, and supported by Jackson, who walk'd by him. And was at last carried before Sheerman, who supported him by a Cord tyed round his Breast. When they came to a Lane called Conduit Lane, in Rogate Parish in this County, Galley in the Extremity of Anguish, cried out, *I shall fall, I shall fall;* upon which Sheerman swore, *Damn you, if you will fall, do then*; and as Galley was falling he gave him a Thrust to the Ground; after which Galley was never seen to move, or heard to speak more.

Jackson, Carter, and the others, in order to prevent a Discovery of the Murder of Galley, went about One of the Clock on the Monday Morning to the Red Lion at Rake in Sussex, a Publick House kept by William Scardefield, whither they carried Chater all over Blood, and with his Eyes almost beat out; and also brought the Body of Galley. They oblig'd Scardefield to shew them a proper Place for the Burial of Galley; and accordingly he went with Carter, Howard, and Steel, to an old Fox Earth, on the Side of a Hill near Rake, at a Place called Harting Comb, where they dug a Hole and buried Galley.

The same Morning, and long before it was Light, whilst some were employed in the Burial of Galley, Jackson and Sheerman carried Chater to the House of Richard Mills the Elder, at Trotten.

I am now come to the third Period of Time; from Chater's Arrival at the House of Richard Mills the Elder, to his Murder upon Wednesday Night the 17th of February.

And it is, that Richard Mills the Elder, first appears to be privy, and consenting to the intended Murder of Chater. A Private House was thought much more proper and safe for the Confinement of Chater, than a Publick House, at all Times open to every Man; and therefore Chater was to be removed from Scardefield's. The Prisoners and their Companions being no Strangers to Old Mills, but his intimate Acquaintance, and Confederates in Smuggling; where could Chater be so secretly imprisoned, as at the Private House of the Elder Mills? And where could he be more securely guarded, than under the Roof of one of their Gang? With these Hopes and Reliance, and in full Confidence of the Secrecy and Assistance of Old Mills, Chater was brought to his House by Jackson and Sheerman; when they came there, they told old Mills they had got a Prisoner; he must get up, and let them in; upon which Old Mills got up, and received

ceived Chater as his Prisoner ; whose Face was then a Gore of Blood, many of his Teeth beat out, his Eyes swelled, and one almost destroyed. I shall here omit one or two particular Circumstances, which the Witnesses will give an Account of ; which shew that Old Mills also was void of all Tenderness and Compassion.

Chater was received by him as a Prisoner, and a Criminal ; and therefore was to be treated as such. Old Mills's House itself was thought too good a Prison for him ; and therefore he was soon dragg'd into a Skeeling or Out-house, adjoining to the House ; wherein Lumber and Fuel was kept. And though Chater was in so weak and deplorable a Condition, as to be scarce able to stand ; yet to prevent all Chance and Possibility of his Escape, he was chained by the Leg with an Iron Chain, fasten'd to a Beam of the Out-house. He was guarded Night and Day ; sometimes by Sheerman, and sometimes by Howard, who came there that Monday Evening. Thus he continued in Chains, until he was loosened for his Execution. But least he should die for want of Sustenance, and disappoint their wicked Designs, he was to be fed, and just kept alive, until the Time and Manner of his Death was determined. During the whole Time of this Imprisonment, Old Mills was at Home, and in his Business as usual. He betrayed not the Trust reposed in him. He acquainted nobody with what had happened, nor with whom

whom he was intrusted. But like a Gaoler, took Care to produce his Prisoner for Execution.

On Wednesday the 17th of February, there was a general Summons of all the Smugglers then in the Neighbourhood, at Scardefield's House, who had been concern'd in breaking open the Custom-House at Poole, to meet that Day at Scardefield's. Upon which Notice, all the Prisoners (except Old Mills) came that Day to Scardefield's. And there were also present John Mills, another Son of Old Mills, Edmund Richards, Thomas Willis, Thomas Stringer, Daniel Perryer, William Steel, and John Raiss; Howard and Sheerman still continuing at Old Mills's, and there guarding Chater. It was at this Consultation at Scardefield's unanimously agreed by all present, that Chater should be murder'd.

This was a deliberate, serious, and determin'd Act of Minds wickedly and cruelly disposed, and executed with all the imaginable Circumstances of Barbarity.

At this Meeting Tapner, Cobby, and Hammond were first concern'd in, and became privy and consenting to this Murder. And there also Richard Mills the Younger first became an Accessary to this Murder: But he was so eager in the Pursuit of it, that he particularly advised and recommended it; and said, he would go with them to the Execution, but he had no Horse. And when he was told, that

that the Old Man (meaning Chater) was carried by a steep Place in the Road to Rake, he said ——*If I had been there, I should have called a Council of War, and he should have come no farther.*

About Eight of the Clock of that Wednesday Evening, all who were present at the Consultation at Scardefield's (except Richard Mills the Younger, John Mills, and Thomas Willis) went from Scardefield's to the House of Old Mills, where they found Chater chained, and guarded by Howard and Sheerman.

They told him he must die, and ordered him to say his Prayers. And whilst he was upon his Knees at Prayers, Cobby kick'd him; and Tapner impatient of Chater's Blood, pulled out a large Clasp Knife, and swore he would be his Butcher, and cut him twice or thrice down the Face, and across his Eyes and Nose. But Old Mills, in Hopes of avoiding the Punishment due to his Guilt, by shifting Chater's Execution to another Place, said—*Don't murder him here, carry him somewhere else first.*

He was then loosened from his Chains, and was by all the Prisoners (except Mills the Father and the Son) and by all the Gang that came from Scardefield's, carried back to that Well, wherein Galley had before been threatn'd to be thrown alive. Jackson and Carter left the Company some small Distance before the other came to the Well; but described the Well to be fenced round with Pales, and directed

rected them where to find it; and said, *We have done our Parts;* meaning, we have murdered Galley; *and you shall do your Parts,* meaning, you shall murder Chater.

Tapner, in order to make good what he had before said, (and happy had it been for him, had he shewn more Regard to his Actions, and less to his Words) after Chater had been forced over the Pales which fenced the Well, pulled a Rope out of his Pocket, put it about Chater's Neck, fastened the other End to the Pales, and there he hung Chater in the Well, until he was dead, as they all imagin'd.

They then loosen'd the Cord from the Rail of the Pales, and let him fall to the Bottom of this Well, which was dry, and one of the Accomplices imagin'd he heard Chater breathe, and that there were still some Remains of Life in him.

To put an End to a Life so miserable and wretched, they threw Pales and Stones upon him. This was the only Act that had any Appearance of Mercy and Compassion; and it brings to my Remembrance, the Saying of the wisest of Men, fully verified in this fatal Instance of Chater's Murder—*The Mercies of the Wicked are Cruelties.*

I am now come to the fourth and last Period of Time.

And here it is observable, that although Providence had for many Months permitted this Murder to remain undiscovered, yet it

was

was then disclosed and brought to Light, when the appointed Time was come, and an Opportunity given to apprehend and bring to Justice many of the Principal Offenders.

Upon the 17th of September last Search was made, in Pursuance of Information given, for the Body of Chater. And the Body was found with a Rope about its Neck, covered with Pales, Stones, and Earth, in that Well I before mentioned, close by Lady Holt Park, in a Wood call'd Harrass Wood, belonging to Mr. Carryll.

By the Length of Time, from February to September, the Body was too much emaciated to be known with any Certainty. But by his Boots, Cloaths, and Belt, there also found, it evidently appeared to be the Body of the unfortunate Chater.

I have now opened to you the Substance of all the most material Facts; and should the Proofs support the Truth of those Facts, no Man can doubt the Consequence thereof, that Chater was murdered, and that the Prisoners were his Murderers.

Mr. Smythe, another of the King's Counsel, also spoke as follows, viz. May it please your Lordships, and Gentlemen of the Jury, I am likewise of Council against the Prisoners at the Bar, three of whom are indicted as Principals for the Murder of Daniel Chater, the other four as Accessaries before the Fact to that Murder.

The Crime they are charged with, is one of the greatest that can be committed against the Laws of God and Man, and in this particular Case attended with the most aggravating Circumstances.

It was not done in the Heat of Passion, and on Provocation, but in cold Blood, deliberately, on the fullest Consideration, in the most cruel Manner, and without any Provocation. The Occasion being as you have heard, only because he dared to speak the Truth, he had seen Dimer passing through Fordingbridge, and had made Oath of it before a Magistrate, being required so to do.

This Prosecution, therefore, is of the utmost Importance to the publick Justice of the Nation, and to the Safety and Security of every Person; not only in this County, but in the Kingdom; for if such Offenders should escape with Impunity, the Consequence would be, that no Crime could be punished. It would teach Highwaymen, Housebreakers, and all other Criminals, to unite in the Manner those Men have done, and whoever received Injuries from them, would not dare complain, or take any Steps towards bringing them to Justice, for Fear of exposing themselves to the Resentment and Revenge of their Companions.

Our Constitution therefore, which must be supported by a regular Administration of Justice, and a due Execution of our Laws, depends

[91]

pends, in some Measure, on bringing such Offenders to condign Punishment; and 'tis to be hoped a few Examples of this Kind will restore the Peace and Tranquility of this Country.

In shortly stating the Facts, I shall endeavour to point out to you the Share which every one of the Persons at the Bar had in this Murder.

In October 1747, the Custom-house at Poole was broke open; the Smugglers who did it, in their Return, passed thro' Fordingbridge, a Town in Hampshire, where Chater saw Dimer among them; and having declared so, was obliged to make Oath of it before a Magistrate; on which Information Dimer was taken up and committed to Chichester Goal for further Examination; and on the 14th of February, Chater was sent by the Collector of Southampton, in Company with Galley, with a Letter to Mr. Battine, Surveyor-General of the Customs, in order that Chater might see if the Man in Chichester Goal was the same Person he saw at Fordingbridge.

These two Men having enquired their Way at the New Inn at Leigh, one Jenkes undertook to direct them, and carried them to the Widow Paine's, at Rowland's Castle, who saying she feared they were going to do the Smugglers some Mischief, sent for Carter and Jacksan, Steel, Raise, Richards, Sheerman, and Howard, who having made Galley and Chater drunk,

drunk, and seen the Letter to Mr. Battine, consulted what to do with them. Some proposed to murder them, others to send them Prisoners to France, and others to confine them, till they saw what became of Dimer, and to treat them as he was dealt with.

Carter and Jackson having sent Jenkes away, this poor Man and Galley were left absolutely in the Power of them and the Smugglers; and indeed, into worse Hands he could not have fallen; had he been taken Prisoner in Battle by our Enemies, he would have had Quarter, and been treated with Humanity; had he fallen into the Hands of Enemies of those Nations who give no Quarter, his Lot would have been immediate Death; but as it was his hard Fate to fall into the Hands of Smugglers, he was to have neither Quarter or immediate Death, but was reserv'd to suffer the most cruel Usage for several Days, and afterwards murdered.

These poor Wretches, after having been beat and abused at Paine's by Carter and Jackson, and the rest of the Gang, were carried away by Force, both set on one Horse with their Legs tied under the Horse's Belly, and whipt and beat by Direction of Carter and Jackson, till they fell; then they were set up again in the same Manner, and whipt and beat again, till they fell a second Time; and were then set on separate Horses, and used in the same Manner, till Galley had the good Fortune

tune to be delivered by Death from their Cruelty; after which they carried Chater, who was bloody, and mangled with the Blows and Falls he had received, to Scardefield's, at the Red Lion at Rake, who observed Jackson's Coat and Hands bloody; and while Carter and the rest buried Galley, Jackson and Sheerman carried Chater to old Mills's in the Night, between the 14th and 15th of February, where he was chained by the Leg in the Skeeling, or Out-house, till the Wednesday Night following, and Sheerman and Howard guarded him.

Imagine to yourselves the Condition of this unhappy Man, certain to die by their Hands, uncertain only as to the Time, and the cruel Manner of it; suffering for three Days and three Nights Pain, Cold, and Hunger; and what was infinitely worse, that Terror and Anxiety of Mind which one in his Situation must continually labour under; he must doubtless envy the Condition of his Companion Galley, who by an early Death was delivered from the Misery he then endured.

On Wednesday following, being the 17th of February, all the Prisoners at the Bar (except old Mills) met at Scardefield's, and there were present also seven more; at which Meeting they consulted what to do with Chater, and it was unanimously agreed by all the thirteen then present, to murder Chater; and young Mills, the Prisoner at the Bar, particularly
ad-

advised it; and said, if he had a Horse, he would go with them to do it; and either then, or at another Meeting at Scardefield's, when Carter and Jackson said, that as they came along, they brought Chater by a steep Place thirty Feet deep, young Mills said, If I had been there, I would have called a Council of War, and he should have come no further.

This being determined, the Prisoners Tapner, Cobby, Hammond, Carter, and Jackson, together with five more of that Company, went to old Mills's, where they found Chater chained, and guarded by Sheerman and Howard, and told him he must die; he said he expected no other; Tapner then said he would be his Butcher, and taking out a Knife, cut him cross the Eyes and Nose; on which old Mills said, *Don't murder him here, but take him somewhere else first.*

Tapner, Cobby, Hammond, Carter, Jackson, and the rest, who came there together, with Sheerman and Howard, then carried him away to murder him; Sheerman, Howard, and Richards, having been concerned in Galley's Murder, said the rest should kill Chater, and therefore went away at Harting; Carter and Jackson having been likewise concerned in Galley's murder, when they came to Lady Holt Park Gate, turned in there, and left the others; having first told them, the Well is a little Way off, you can't miss it, 'tis fenced round

round with Pales, to keep the Cattle from falling in.

Tapner, Cobby, Hammond, Carter, Jackson, and the rest, went then to the Well, where Tapner put a Rope about Chater's Neck to hang him; and some of the Pales being broken down, Chater would have crept through, Tapner would not let him, but made him climb over the Pales, weak as he was, and then hanged him in the Well about a Quarter of an Hour, till they thought him dead; then having drawn him up till they could take hold of his Legs, they threw him headlong into the Well; and fancying they heard him breathe or groan, threw Posts and Stones in upon him, and went their Way.

The Terror this Act of Cruelty had spread through the Country, stopt every Person's Mouth, who had it in their Power to give any Information; so that the Body was not to be found till September last, when it was so putrified and consumed, as not to be known but by the Belt which was about it, and which Chater's Wife will prove to be her Husband's. If there was any Doubt as to the Identity of the Man, we could shew likewise, that being examined by the Smugglers just before he was murdered, he said his Name was Daniel Chater.

It appears therefore from this State of the Case, that all the Prisoners are guilty of the Indictment; Tapner was present at the Consultation,

sultation at Scardefield's, and was the Person who hanged him; Cobby and Hammond were present at the Consultation, helped to carry him to the Well, and were present at the Murder, and therefore equally guilty with Tapner as Principals. Carter and Jackson took him away by Force from Pain's, and by the Treatment of him there and on the Road, shewed an Intention from the first to murder him, though perhaps the particular Death he was to suffer, was not then agreed on; they were afterwards present at the Consultation at Scardefield's, where it was resolved to murder him, and went almost to the Well with him; and when they parted, gave those who murder'd him particular Directions to the Well. Young Mills was also at the Consultation, and particularly advised and directed the Murder, in which he declared he would have joined, if he had a Horse. Old Mills, though he kept no Publick House, and therefore was not obliged to receive Guests, receives this Man brought in the Night, in a bloody and deplorable Condition. Chater is chained in his Out-house from Sunday Night till Wednesday; yet Old Mills never discovers it to any Person, or uses any Means to deliver him, which is a strong Evidence of his Knowledge and Approbation of their Design; and when Tapner declared he would be his Butcher and cut him, Old Mills expresses no Disapprobation of the Murder, does not dissuade

dissuade him from it, but desires him *not to do it there, but carry him somewhere else first,* which shews his Approbation of the Fact; though to secure himself, as he thought, from Punishment, he would have had it committed at some other Place.

This, Gentlemen, is the Fact, which shews that securing themselves and their Companions was not their principal Aim; were it so, they would have murder'd this Man as soon as they had him in their Power; but their Motive seems to have been Revenge, and a Disposition to torture one, who should dare to give any Information, which might bring them or their Friends into Danger.

After hearing the whole Evidence, if these Men appear innocent, God forbid they should be found guilty; and I would not have the cruel Circumstances of the Fact incline you to believe any Thing we suggest, that is not supported by the strongest Proof: But if the Fact is proved beyond a Possibility of Doubt, to be in the Manner we have stated it, I am sure you will do your Duty, and by a just and honest Verdict, deliver your Country from Men so void of Humanity.

The King's Counsel having finished what they had to premise to the Court and Jury, which we have already related, they then proceeded to call the Witnesses for the Crown in support of the Charge against the Prisoners; the first Witness called was Mr. Milner, Collector

lector of the Customs at the Port of Pool, who deposed, that about the 17th of October, 1747, he had Advice that the Custom-house at Pool was broke open; upon which he hastened thither, and found the outer Door burst open, and the other Door broke in Pieces; that the Room wherein some Run Tea was lodged, was taken by Capain Johnson, was broke open, and all the Tea carried away, excepting a little Bag, containing about four or five Pounds.

Mr. Sheerer, Collector of the Customs at Southampton, was next call'd, who deposed that in February last he received a Letter from the Commissioners of the Customs, acquainting him, that one John Dimer was committed to Chichester Goal, on Suspicion of breaking open the Custom-house at Pool, with Directions to send the deceas'd Daniel Chater, who could give some Information against Dimer, to Justice Battine, the Surveyor-General, and to acquaint Justice Battine with the Occasion of his sending Chater; that he accordingly sent Chater with a Letter addressed to Justice Battine, under the Care of one William Galley, a Tidesman in the Port of Southampton; that they set out on Sunday Morning the 14th of February last; he could not take upon him to say how Chater was dress'd, but he remembered he rode upon a dark brown Horse, and had a Great Coat on, with another Coat under it, and upon the under Coat a Belt; he could not

[99]

not recollect how Galley was dressed, but remember'd that he was mounted upon a grey Horse.

The next Witness call'd and sworn was William Galley, the Son of the deceas'd William Galley, who deposed, that he remembered his Father's setting out upon this Journey to Justice Battine, in February last; that he saw the Letter to Justice Battine the Night before his Father set out, and saw the Directions; he remembered the Dress his Father had on; it was a blue Great Coat, with brass Buttons covered with blue, a close-bodied Coat, of a light brown Colour, lined with blue, with a Waistcoat and Breeches of the same, and that he rode on a grey Horse; he remembered that Daniel Chater a Shoemaker of Fordingbridge set out at the same Time with his Father, and had on a light Surtout Coat, with red Breeches, and a Belt round him, and rode upon a brown Horse; that this was the last Time he ever saw his Father alive, and that he never saw Chater since.

Edward Holton was next call'd and sworn, who deposed, that on the 14th of February last he saw Daniel Chater and another Person, whom he took to be Mr. Galley, at his own House, at Havant, in the County of Hants; that he knew Chater very well, and had some Conversation with him; that Chater told him he was going to Chichester upon a little Business; and then went out to Galley, and brought in a Letter,

ter, which was directed to William Battine, Esq; at East Marden; upon which he (the Witness) told him, he was going out of his Way; that Galley wished he would direct them the Way; that he directed them to go thro' Stanstead, near Rowland's Castle; and that they said they should be back again the next Day.

George Austen being call'd and sworn, deposed, that on Sunday the 14th of February last he saw two Men, one mounted upon a brown Horse, and the other upon a Grey, at the New Inn at Leigh, in the Parish of Havant; that they came to the New Inn when he was there, and inquired the Way to East Marden; to which Place he was going to direct them, when one of the Men, who had a blue Coat on, pulled a Letter out of his Pocket, which he (the Witness) looked at, and seeing it was directed to Justice Battine at East Marden, he told them they were going ten Miles out of the Way; and that he and his Brother Thomas Austen, and his Brother-in-Law Robert Jenkes, were going Part of their Road, and would conduct them the best they could; that they went no further together than to a Place call'd Rowland's Castle, to a Publick House which was kept by the Widow Paine; the two Strangers Galley and Chater call'd for Rum at the Widow Paine's. This was about the Middle of the Day, or something after. That the Widow Paine asked him if he knew these
Men,

[101]

Men, or whether they belonged to his Company; he told her they were going to Justice Battine's, and that he was going to shew them the Way; she then said she thought they were going to do Harm to the Smugglers, and desir'd him to set them out of the Way, which he refused to do; she then seemed uneasy, and she and her Son consulted together; that her Son went out, and the Prisoner Jackson came in in a little Time; that the Prisoner Carter, and several more, came thither soon afterwards. He knew none but Jackson and Carter. * That Jackson enquired where the two Men were bound for, and the Man in the light Coat answered, they were going to Justice Battine's, and from thence to Chichester; but Carter was not by at that Time; that Galley and Chater had some Rum, and Jackson call'd for a Mug of Hot, which was Gin and Beer mixed, or something of that Kind, and to the best of his Knowledge they all drank together; he did not see any ill Treatment, nor either of the Men bloody whilst he was there; that he went away between Two and Three, and left the two Men there; the Widow Paine call'd him out of Doors, and told him his Brother Jenkes wanted to speak to him; when he came out, his Horse was at the Hedge by the back Door, and his Brother said
he

---

* The other five Prisoners were not at Rowland's Castle, so that Mr. Austin could have no Knowledge of them.

[102]

he wondered why the two Men did not go away; upon which he went back again into the House, and his Brother was uneasy because he did so; that the Widow Paine advised him to go Home, and said the two Men would be directed the Way; he was uneasy at going without them, because he saw so many Men come in, and imagined they had a Design to do some Harm to them; that when he went away, Jackson and Carter were left with the two Men, Galley and Chater, to the best of his Knowledge; and Jackson, as well as the Widow Paine, persuaded him to go Home, saying it would be better for him. He was positive that Jackson and Carter were there, for he knew them very well.

The Court asked Jackson and Carter, if they would ask this Witness any Questions.

To which they both answered, they had no Questions to ask him.

Thomas Austen was then call'd, who deposed, that he was at the New Inn at Leigh on Valentine's Day last, with his Brother George, where he saw two Men who enquired the Way to Justice Battine's; he went from thence with them to Rowland's Castle; they went to the Widow Paine's at that Place, and called for a Dram of Rum; the Prisoners were not there at first, but in a little Time Jackson came; and soon afterwards the Prisoner Carter. That the Widow Paine spoke to him at the outer Door before either of the Prisoners came, and
ask'd

ask'd him if he knew the two Men, and said she was afraid they were come to do the Smugglers some Mischief, and that she would send for William Jackson; accordingly her Son went for him, and he soon came, and another little Man and his Servant. This Witness further deposed, that he saw in the House one Joseph Southern, and the Prisoner Carter, but that Carter did not come so soon as Jackson; that Jackson struck one of the Men who had a blue Coat on, but they were all soon appeas'd, and then they all drank very freely, and he was drunk and went to sleep, and the two Men were fuddled and went to sleep in the little Room ; that about 7 o'Clock Jackson went into the Room and waked the two Men ; after they came out, the two Men were taken away by Jackson and Carter, and one William Steel, and Edmund Richards; but he did not remember they were forced away, and did not see them upon the Horses, nor did he ever see them any more ; this was between 7 and 8 o'Clock.

Being ask'd whether he saw either of the Men produce his Deputation or heard any high Words.

He said he did not ; that he was asleep the best Part of the Afternoon, and did not see any ill Treatment, but that one Blow which he had mentioned.

Being

Being cross-examin'd at the Request of the Prisoners,

He depos'd, that he did not know who the two Strangers were, but they were the same two Persons that his Brother George had just spoke of, and had a Letter for Justice Battine; that one of them had a blue Coat on, and rode upon a grey Horse, and the other Man rode upon a brownish Horse; that he did not see the Direction of the Letter, but he heard it read by Robert Jenkes.

The next Witness produced was Robert Jenkes, who came with the two deceas'd Men from Leigh to this House, along with the two Brothers, George and Thomas Austen, who being sworn, deposed, that he saw two Men upon the 14th of February last, at the New Inn at Leigh, one of them upon a brownish Horse, the other upon a grey, and dressed in Riding Coats; that they were the same Men that the Witnesses George & Thomas Austen had spoke of; that they all went together to Rowland's Castle, and got there about 12 o'Clock, or something after, and went into a House there which was kept by the Widow Paine; he did not hear her give any Directions to send for any body; but the Prisoners Carter and Jackson soon came thither; that whilst he was there he did not see any Abuse, or observe that either of them were bloody; and that he had no Conversation with Jackson further than that

that Jackson said he would see the Letter, which was going to Major Battine, and Carter he believed might say so too; when he wanted to go away Jackson would not suffer him to go through the Room where the two Men were (for the two Men were carried into another Room) but Jackson told him if he had a Mind to go he might go through the Garden to the back Part of the House, where his Horse should be led ready for him; that he did so, and found his Horse there and went away.

Being now particularly ask'd if he could say why Jackson refus'd his going through the Room where the two Men were, he answer'd he could not be certain, but believed it was for fear the two Men should go away with him; and that he did not order his Horse to be led round to the Garden himself; and that George Austen and he went away together upon his Horse, and that Jackson declared he would see the Letter one of the Men had in his Pocket; and the Witness saw the Direction of it was to William Battine, Esq; at East Marden.

Being cross-examined by the Prisoner Carter, whether Carter said he would see the Letter, he answered that both Carter and Jackson said they would see the Letter for Justice Battine; that he [the Witness] did not order his Horse to be carried to the back Part of the House; and that Carter was by when he was told by Jackson, that if he had a Mind to go, his Horse

P   should

should be led to the back Part of the House.

Joseph Southern was then call'd and sworn, who depos'd that on Sunday the 14th of February last, he saw Jenkes, the two Austens, and two other Men on the Road coming from Havant towards Rowland's Castle, one of them had a blue Coat on, and rode a grey Horse; that he went to Rowland's Castle himself that Day, and saw Jenkes, the two Austens, and the same two Men sitting on Horseback drinking at the Widow Paine's Door ; he staid there best Part of an Hour, and saw them and several other Persons in the House ; that he saw the Prisoners Carter and Jackson in the House whilst he staid there; he sat down and drank a Pint of Beer by the Kitchen Fire, but the other Persons were in another Room; that he saw the two Men come out to the Door and go in again, and one of them had an Handkerchief over his Eye, and there was Blood upon it ; that he met this Man as he was going in, and heard him say to Jackson, *I am the King's Officer, and I will take Notice of you that struck me.* That Carter was not present when this was said, but was in the House; the Man who spoke thus to Jackson had a Parchment in his Hand when he met him at the Door ; he likewise saw a Letter in his Hand, and heard him say he was going to Justice Battine with it; and that he (the Witness) went away between 2 and 3 o'Clock, and did not know what became of the Letter, nor had he heard

heard either Jackson or Carter say what became of it.

This being all Mr. Southern had to say, and Jackson and Carter, tho' asked particularly if they would have him ask'd any Questions, saying they had none, he was set down.

And then William Garret was sworn, who deposed that he was at the Widow Paine's on the 14th of February last about 4 o'Clock in the Afternoon, and saw the Prisoners Jackson and Carter and two Strangers there; that one of them, who had a blue Coat on, had received a Stroke upon his Cheek, and the Blood run down it; that just as he came in, this Man was standing up by the Back of a Chair, and Jackson stood by him, and he heard Jackson say, *That for a Quartern of Gin he would serve him so again*, by which the Witness understood that Jackson had struck him before. He did not hear the Man say he was the King's Officer, but he heard Jackson say, *You a King's Officer! I'll make you a King's Officer, and that you shall know.* That when he went away, he left them all there.

The Prisoners would not ask this Witness any Questions.

The next Witness produced was William Lamb, who being sworn deposed, That he went to the Widow Paine's, at Rowland's Castle on the 14th of February last about Four in the Afternoon, and found Jackson and Carter

Carter there; that before he went, he saw one of the Widow Paine's Sons call Carter aside, at his House at West-Bourne; that there were several other People there (Rowland's Castle) in another Room, amongst whom were Thomas Austen, and two Men that were Strangers to him, one of whom had on a blue Great Coat; he further deposed that the two Men who were Strangers, he understood, were going with a Letter to Justice Battine; but that he saw no ill Treatment, during the little Time he staid there; that during the Time he was there he said, Edmund Richards, one of the Company, pull'd out a Pistol, and said, *That whoever should discover any thing that passed at that House he would blow his Brains out.* But that Jackson and Carter, two of the Prisoners, were not in the Room when these Words were spoken, as he verily believes. He saw, he said, the Man in the blue Great Coat pull a Parchment out of his Pocket, and heard him tell the People he was the King's Officer; his Wig was then off, and there was Blood upon his Cheek; that he saw a Letter, which he understood to be going to Mr. Battine; one Kelly, and the Prisoner Carter, had it in their Hands, but he did not know how they came by it; that he did not see the Direction of the Letter; but he observ'd it was broke open, when he saw it in the Hands of Carter and Kelly; and he understood, by the Discourse of the Company, that it was a Letter

[109]

ter which the two Strangers were to carry to Mr. Battine, but he never heard it read.

The Prisoners, Carter and Jackson, would not ask him any Questions.

Richard Kent deposed, that he was at the Widow Paine's on the 14th of February last; that he saw the Prisoners Jackson and Carter, and many others there, particularly two Strangers, who he supposed were the two unfortunate Men Galley and Chater; that they took the two Strangers out with them, and that Edmund Richards told him, that if he spoke a Word of what he had heard or seen there, he would shoot him thro' the Body; but Jackson and Carter were not in the Room when Richards said this.

George Poate was next call'd, who deposed, that he was at Rowland's Castle on Sunday the 14th of February last, about seven o'Clock in the evening, or after; and saw nine Men there, and that the Prisoners, Jackson and Carter, were two of them; he staid there about half an Hour, and as soon as he came in, he saw four or five Men with Great Coats and Boots on, most of them upon their Legs, as if they were just going; he went and warmed himself by the Kitchen Fire, and called for a Pint of Beer, and soon after he heard the Stroke of a Whip repeated three or four Times, in a little Room that was at the Corner of the Kitchen, but did not see who gave the Blows, nor who received them; that he afterwards

terwards heard a strange Rustling of People, more than before, and saw seven or eight Men come into the Kitchen; that he knew the Prisoners, Jackson and Carter, and William Steele, Edmund Richards, and two that went by the Names of Little Sam and Little Harry; there were two other Persons there, whom, to his Knowledge, he had never seen before nor since, and could give no Account of them, nor did he observe how they were dress'd; that soon after he thought he heard a Blow, and he saw Jackson in a moving Posture, as if he had just given a Blow, and was drawing up his Arm in a proper Form, as if he was going to give another; but William Paine stepp'd up, and called him Fool and Blockhead for so doing; upon which he sunk his Arm, and did not behave in the like Manner any more, in his Sight; that just as they were going out of Doors, Jackson turned round, with a Pistol in his Hand, and asked for a Belt, a Strap, or String, but nobody gave him either, and he put his Pistol into his Great Coat Pocket, and went away with the rest; that by the trampling of Horses, he supposed they all went on Horseback, but which Way he knew not; it was between seven and eight o'Clock, as nigh as he could guess, when they went off; he did not hear any Conversation about one of the Strangers being the King's Officer, nor did he see the Blow given, nor the Person to whom the other Blow was going to be given.

The

[111]

The Prisoners Jackson and Carter said they had no Questions to ask this Witness.

Then his Majesty's Counsel desired that John Rase otherwise Raise, he being an Accessary in the Fact, who appearing and being sworn, deposed, That on Sunday the 14th of February he was at Rowland's Castle, between twelve and one o'Clock at Noon ; that when he came there he found Edmund Richards, William Steel, the Prisoners, Carter, Jackson, and Little Sam, Richard Kelly, Jackson's Wife, & Galley & Chater ; he saw Jackson take Chater to the Door, and heard him ask him if he knew any Thing of Dimar the Shepherd, and Chater answer'd he did, and was obliged to go and speak against him ; that Galley then went out to keep Chater from talking to Jackson ; whereupon Jackson knocked Galley down with his Fist ; that Galley came in again, & soon after Jackson and Carter. When they were all come in, he (the Witness) with the Prisoners, Jackson and Carter, and Edmund Richards, went into the back Room ; that there they enquir'd of Jackson what he had got out of the Shoemaker (meaning Daniel Chater;) that Jackson informed them, that Chater said he knew Dimar, & was obliged to come in as a Witness against him ; that then they consulted what to do with them (Chater and Galley) this was about Three o'Clock in the Afternoon : They first proposed to carry them to some secure Place, where they might be taken Care of till they

had

had an Opportunity of carrying them over to France; and that when this Proposition was made the Prisoners, Jackson and Carter, and Richards and himself were present. This Resolution was taken to send them out of the Way, that Chater should not appear against Dimar; and afterwards it was agreed to fetch a Horse and carry them away: That Galley and Chater appeared very uneasy; and wanted to be gone; and thereupon Jackson's Wife, to pacify them, told them that she lived at Major Battine's, and her Horse was gone for, and as soon as it came she would shew them the Way to Mr. Battine's; that he (the Witness) then went away, and saw no more of them that Night.

Being cross-examined, at the Request of the Defendants Counsel, said, At this Consultation there was nothing mentioned, as he remembered then, but the securing them, in order to carry them to France.

This Witness having gone thus far in his Evidence, was set by for the present; the Counsel for the Crown declaring that they would call him again, to give an Account of what passed on the 17th, when Chater was murdered; after they had examined the next Witness.

Then William Steel, one of the Accomplices in both the Murders from Beginning to End, was call'd and sworn, who deposed, that he was sent for to the Widow Paine's on Sunday the

the 14th of February; that the Prisoner Jackson, Little Sam, one Kelly, and two Men more, and Jackson's Wife, were there when he came, which was about two o'Clock in the Afternoon, and soon afterwards Little Harry, the Prisoner Carter, Edmund Richards, John Raise the last Witness, and Carter's Wife, came thither; he said he did not know how Carter or Jackson came to be there, but the Widow Paine's Son came and called him (the Witness) out, and said he must go to the Castle, his Mother's, for there were two Men come to swear against the Shepherd, meaning John Dimer; that when he came in he found the two Strangers, Galley and Chater, and the Prisoners Jackson, Carter, Richards and some others; and that they were in general sober, as far as he saw, but they sat drinking together about two Hours; that Jackson took Chater out of the House, to examine him about Dimer, and after they had been out some Time, Galley seeming all the Time very uneasy, went out to them, but soon returned, and said Jackson had knocked him down; the Witness saw he was bloody all down the left Cheek; that Jackson wa; not in the Room when Galley came in, but came in with Carter a little Time afterwards: That then Galley, addressing himself to Jackson, said he did not know any Occasion Jackson had to use him in that Manner, and that he should remember it, and took down his Name in

Q

Jack-

Jackson's Presence. Galley likewise said he was an Officer, and shewed his Deputation to the People that were in the Room.

Galley and Chater, this Witness continuing his Deposition, said, began to be very uneasy, and wanted to be going, but that the Prisoners, Jackson and Carter, and the rest of them that were Smugglers, persuaded them to stay, and be pacify'd, and all Things should be set right, and the Company continued drinking till Galley and Chater were quite fuddled, and were carried into a little inner Room to sleep; this was about Four or Five o'Clock, and they continued in the little Room two or three Hours; the rest of the Company sat drinking all the while, consulting what to do with Galley and Chater. The Prisoners Jackson and Carter, and Little Sam, Little Harry, Richards, and the Witness, were at this Consultation. It was proposed to put them (Galley and Chater) out of the Way, because they should not appear against the Shepherd, meaning Dimar; after which it was proposed to throw them into the Well in the Horse Pasture, about a Quarter of a Mile from Rowland's Castle, but that was thought not convenient to put them into a well so near, for fear of a Discovery.

Here the Question was particularly ask'd Steel the Witness, which of them it was that proposed the murdering them directly, and flinging them afterwards down the Well; to which

which he reply'd *he believed he might.*

After this it was next proposed to join, and each Man to allow them Threepence a Week, and to keep them in some secret Place, till they saw what became of Dimar, and as Dimar was served, so these two People (Chater and Galley) were to be served; this was talked of while Chater and Galley were asleep, and there was no other Proposal made as he heard at that Time: But while they were talking these Things, the Wives of Carter and Jackson said it was no Matter what became of them (Galley and Chater) or what was to be done to them; they ought to be hanged, for they were come to ruin them, meaning the Smugglers: He then said, that about Seven o'Clock Carter and Jackson went into the inner Room, and waked Galley and Chater, and brought them out of the Room, very bloody and very drunk; he did not see what pass'd in the Room, but was sure they did not go in so bloody; and he believed Jackson and Carter had kicked and spurred them, for they had put on their Boots and Spurs; that then Jackson and Carter brought them (Galley & Chater) out into the Kitchen; and took them through to the Street Door all very bloody, when they set Galley the Officer upon a brown or black Horse, and Chater up behind him; That Jackson, Carter, and Richards put them on Horseback and tied their Legs under the Horse's Belly, and also tied their Legs together;

ther; then they tied a Line to the Bridle, and he (the Witness) got upon a grey Horse and led them along; that just after they turned round the Corner about 70 or 80 Yards from the House, Jackson cried out, *whip them, lick them Dogs, cut them;* it was then dark, and the Company whipped and lashed them with their Horsewhips, some on one-Side and some on the other, with great Violence, on the Face and Head and other Parts of the Body, and continued doing so while they rode about Half a Mile to a Place called Woodash or Wood's Ashes; that there they alighted, and Little Sam gave all the Company a Dram or two, but none to Galley and Chater; that as they were mounted again Jackson and Carter cried out, *damn them, lick them, whip them,* and they were whipped as before for about a Mile further, and then they fell down under the Horse's Belly with their Heads upon the Ground and their Legs over the Saddle; upon which Jackson and Carter and some of the others of the Gang dismounted, and untied Galley and Chater, and immediately set them up again, and their Legs were tied together in the same Posture; and the Company went on whipping them as before till they came to a Place called * Dean, which was about Half a Mile further; they were beat very much, and in the Judgment

* The Name of the Place is Goodthrop Dean, a little Village.

[117]

ment of the Witness it was almost impossible they should sit their Horses; that when they came to Dean somebody of the Company pulled out a Pistol, and said he would shoot them [Galley & Chater] thro' the Head if they made any Noise whilst they went through the Village; he could not tell who it was that threatned to shoot them but apprehends it was done for fear the People in the Village should hear them; then went on but a Foot Pace, and after they got through Dean, they were whipped again as before, and when they came near a Place called Idsworth they fell down again under the Horse's Belly, and then some of the Company loosed them, and set up the Officer [Galley] behind him, [the Witness] and Chater behind Little Sam, and in this Manner they proceeded towards Lady Holt Park, which is near 3 Miles from Idsworth, whipping Galley and Chater as before, but the Lashes of their Whips falling upon the Witness, as he sat before Galley, he [the Witness] could not bear the Strokes, and therefore he cryed out, and then they left off whipping Galley in that Manner.

This Witness further said, that Galley sat upon the Horse till they got to Lady Holt Park, and then being faint and tired with riding, he got down, and then Carter and Jackson took him one by the Arms and the other by the Legs, and carried him towards a Well called Harris's Well, by the Side of Lady Holt Park;
and

and then Jackson said to Carter, *We'll throw him into the Well,* to which Carter replied *with all my Heart,* and Galley seemed very indifferent what they did with him; but some of the Company saying, 'twas Pity to throw him into the Well, Jackson and Carter set him up behind the Witness again, and Chater was still behind Little Sam; they went on in this Manner till they came to go down a Hill, when Galley was faint and tired, and could not ride any further, and got down there; upon which Carter and Jackson laid him on a Horse before Edmund Richards, with his Belly upon the Pummel of the Saddle. They laid him across the Horse, because he was so bad that they could not contrive to carry him in any other Manner, and they carried him so for about a Mile and a Half from the Well; that then Richards being tired of holding him, let him down the Side of the Horse; and Carter and Jackson put him upon the grey Horse, that he [the Witness] was upon, and the Witness got off; they sat him up, his Legs across the Saddle, and his Body lay over the Horse's Mane; that in this Posture Jackson held him on; and he did not remember that any Body else held him at that Time; that they went on for about Half a Mile in this Manner, Galley crying out vehemently all the Time, *Barbarous Usage! Barbarous Usage! for God's sake shoot me through the Head or through the Body;* he [the Witness] thought Jackson

was

[119]

was at this Time pinching him by the privy Parts, for there were no Blows given when he cried so; that Chater was still with the Company behind Little Sam, and they went on for about two Miles and a Half further, the Company holding Galley by Turns on the Horse, 'till they came to a dirty Lane ; at which Place, Carter and Jackson rode forwards, and bid the rest of the Company stop at the Swing-Gate beyond the Water, till they should return. Jackson and Carter left them here, and went to see for a Place proper for taking Care of Chater and Galley, but soon came to them again at the Swing-Gate, and told them, that the Man of the House, whither they went, was ill, and that they could not go thither; by which he understood that they had been in the Neighbourhood to get Entertainment. It was then proposed to go forward to the House of one Scardefield; & Little Harry tied Galley with a Cord, and got up on Horseback behind him, in order to hold him up on the Horse, and they went on till they came to a gravelly Knap in the Road ; at which Place Galley cried out, *I shall fall, I shall fall* ; whereupon Little Harry said, *D——n you then fall,* and gave him a Push, and Galley fell down and gave a Spirt, and never spoke a Word more ; he [the Witness] believed his Neck was broke by the Fall ; that then they laid him across the Horse again, and went away for Rake, to the Sign of the Red Lion, which

was

[120]

was kept by William Scardefield; that Chater was behind Little Sam, and was carried to Scardefield's House, and was very bloody when they came to Scardefield's; that Jackson and Little Harry went from Scardefield's with Chater about Three o'Cleck in the Morning; and Jackson afterwards returned to Scardefield's, & said he had left Chater at Old Mills's House, and that Little Harry was left to look after him that he might not escape; this was Monday the 15th of February, and they remained all that Day at Scardefield's House; that the Prisoner Richard Mills the younger was there on that Day; and upon hearing from Jackson and Carter that they had passed by a Precipice of about thirty Foot deep, when they had Chater with them, he said, *If I had been there, I would have called a Council of War on the Spot, and he* [Chater] *should have gone no further*; or to that Effect.

That 2 or 3 Days afterwards the Company met at Scardefield's again, to consult what to do with Chater; that the Prisoners John Raiss, Carter and Jackson, the Prisoner Richard Mills the younger, a Son of the Prisoner Richard Mills the elder, Thomas Willis, John Mills, another Son of Old Mills, the Prisoners, Tapner, Cobby, Hammond, and Thomas Stringer, Edmund Richards, and Daniel Perrier, and he [the Witness] were consulting what to do
with

[121]

with Chater, and John Mills * proposed to take him out, and load a Gun, and tie a String to the Trigger, and place him (Chater) against the Gun, and that they should all of them pull the String, to involve every one of them in the same Degree of Guilt; but this Proposal was not agreed to. Then Jackson and Carter proposed to carry him back to the Well near Lady Holt Park, and to murder him there, which was agreed to by all the Company; but Richard Mills the younger and John Mills said, they could not go with them to the Well, because they had no Horses; and as it was in their (the other Persons) Way home, they might do it as well without them; and so it was concluded to murder Chater, and then to throw him into the Well.

As soon as it was agreed amongst them to murder Chater, and fling him down the Well, they went away from Rake to the House of the Prisoner Richard Mills the Elder, & found Chater in a back Skilling, or Out-house, run up at the Back of Mills's House, a Place they usually put Turf in; where they found him chained with an Iron Chain, about three Yards long, to a Beam in the Skilling; that Chater was bloody about the Head, and had a Cut upon one of his Eyes, so that he could not see with it; that the Prisoner, Richard Mills the Elder, was

R   at

---

* The Witness was not certain whether it was John Mills, or his Brother Richard Mills that made the Proposal.

at Home himself, and fetched out Bread and Cheese for them to eat, and gave them Drink, and received them and made them welcome; that the House is a private House, no Inn or Alehouse; that they all of them went to and again, between the House and the Skilling, and that the Prisoner, Richard Mills the Elder, was at Home all the while; that the Prisoner Tapner bid Chater go to Prayers, and pulled out a large clasp Knife, and swore he would be his Butcher, and while Chater was at Prayers he cut him cross his Eyes and Nose, and down his Forehead, so that he bled to a great Degree. He was order'd by some others of the Company to say his Prayers, for they were come to kill him, and kill him they would; and some of the Company were then in the Skilling, and the rest of them were in the House, but no one interposed to save his Life; that he [the Witness] was in the Skilling, when Chater was advised to say his Prayers, and was cut, and that Chater was chained by the Leg at that Time.

When they had kept him there as long as they thought fit, somebody of the Company unlocked the Chain, and set him on Horseback, and John Raiss, Edmund Richards, Little Harry, Little Sam, the Prisoners Tapner, Thomas Stringer, the Prisoners Cobby and Hammond, Daniel Perryer, the Prisoners Jackson, Carter, and the Witness, set out with him for Lady Holt Park, to carry him down to the Well;

Well; that when they came to a Place call'd Harting, Richards, Little Harry, and Little Sam, went back; and when the rest came to the white Gate by Lady Holt Park, Carter and Jackson left them, but first told them they must keep along a little further, and they could not miss the Well, for there were white Pales; that it was about 200 Yards further, and that there were some Pales on the Right Hand of it, and that there were Pales round the Well. They went on, found the Well by the Direction Carter and Jackson had given them, and carried Chater with them; that then Tapner, Hammond, Stringer & Cobby got off their Horses, and Tapner pulled a Cord out of his Pocket, and put it about Chater's Neck, and led him towards the Well. Chater seeing two or three Pales down, said he could get through, but Tapner said, *No, you shall get over*; and he did so, with the Rope about his Neck; they then put him into the Well, and hanged him, winding the Rope round the Rails, and his Body hung down in the Mouth of the Well for about a Quarter of an Hour; and then Stringer took hold of his Legs to pull him aside, and let his Head fall first into the Well, and Tapner let the Rope go, and down fell the Body into the Well Head foremost; that they staid there some Time, and one of the Company said he thought he heard him breathe or groan in the Well; on this they all listened, and being of the same Opinion, they went to one Combleach a Gardener, who was in Bed, but they disturbed him, and asked him to lend them a Ladder and a Rope, for one of their Company had fallen down the Well; which he readily did, not thinking, as the Witness verily believed, any otherwise. They brought the Ladder with them to the Well, but as it was a long one they could not get it down the Well thro' the Hole in the Breach of the Pales; when they all tried to raise it and put it over the Pales, but then not having Strength sufficient they laid that Part of their Design aside; and looking about them found an old Gate Post or two, which they threw into the Well upon him, and then left him.

Steele, the Witness, being cross-examined as to this, said, He never heard the Prisoner say he would not have them murder the Man; and added, That he was sure he must hear them talk of murdering while they were at his House.

John Raiss being called again said, That after he had left the Company at the Widow Paine's, on the 14th of February, as mentioned in the former Part of his Evidence, he met some of the same Company, and others, on the Wednesday Evening following, being the 17th of February at Scardefield's at Rake; that the Prisoners, Richard Mills the Younger, Carter, Jackson, Tapner, Cobby, and Hammond, with Steele, Richards, Little Sam, Daniel Perrier, John Mills, and Thomas Willis, were there; and

and it was proposed at that Meeting to murder Chater. He could not say who first made the Proposal, but, to the best of his Knowledge, it was either Carter or Jackson, and it was agreed to by all the Company; it was not then resolved how it was to be done, but only in general, that he was to be murdered, and thrown into a Well; that they went to the House of the Prisoner, Richard Mills the Elder, to join Little Harry, who was left there to take Care of Chater, and found Chater chained by the Leg upon some Turf in a Skilling, at the Backside of the House; that the Prisoner, Richard Mills the Elder, was at Home, and ordered his Housekeeper to fetch Bread and Cheese, and some Houshold Beer, for any of them to eat and drink that would, and was sure Old Mills knew that they came for Chater; that Tapner and Cobby were very earnest to go and see Chater; and Tapner having his Knife in his Hand said, "*This Knife shall be his Butcher;*" that thereupon the Prisoner Richard Mills the Elder said, "*Pray do not murder him here, but carry him somewhere else before you do it;*" that Old Mills said this, upon seeing that Tapner had his Knife in his Hand, and hearing him declare it should be his (Chater's) Butcher; that they then went out into the Skilling, and found Chater sitting upon some Heath or Turf, and Tapner ordered him to say his Prayers: While he was repeating the Lord's Prayer Tapner cut him

over

over the Face with his Knife, and Cobby stood by, kicking and damning him. This too was whilst the poor Man was saying the Lord's Prayer. That Chater asked them what was become of Galley, and they told him he was murdered, and that they were come to murder him. Upon which Chater earnestly begg'd to live another Day; that Cobby asked him his Name, and whether he had not formerly done Harvest-work at Selsea? To which he answered that his Name was Daniel Chater, and that he had harvested at Selsea, and there be became acquainted with Dimar. That Little Harry unlocked the Horse-lock that was on his (Chater's) Legs, & Tapner, Cobby, and Stringer, brought him out of the Skillin, and set him upon Tapner's Mare, in order to carry him to the Well, to be there murdered, and thrown in; and that all the Company knew, at that Time, what was to be done with him; that they rid about three Miles towards the Well, and sometimes whipt Chater with their Horsewhips; and Tapner observing that he bled, said d——n his Blood, if he blooded his (Tapner's) Saddle, *he would whip him again.* When they came to Harting, Carter, Jackson, Richards, Little Sam, Little Harry, & Steele, said *We have done our Parts, and you (meaning the rest of the Company) shall do yours.* By which they meant, as he took it, that they had murdered Galley, and that the rest should

should murder Chater; and Richards, Little Sam, and Little Harry, stopped there, and did not accompany them any further; the rest went on towards the Well, but Carter and Jackson stopp'd before they came to it, and told them the Well was a little further off, describing it to them, and told them they could not miss finding it, for it had some white Pales by it, and that it was not above 200 Yards farther, and then Jackson and Carter left them; that he [the Witness] & Tapner, Cobby, Stringer, Hammond, Perryer & Steele, came to the Well, got off their Horses, and took Chater off his Horse, the Witness was not certain which, and either Tapner or Cobby put a Cord round his Neck; that there was a Shord in the Pales about the Well, and he heard Chater say he could get through there, but Cobby or Tapner said, *Damn you, no, you shall not, you shall get over*; that Tapner wound the Cord round the Pales, and Chater being put into the Mouth of the Well, hung by the Neck for about a quarter of an Hour, and then they loosened the Rope, and turned the Body, that it fell into the Well Head foremost. They staid there till some of the Company thought they heard him breathe or groan, and then went to get a Rope and a Ladder at one Combleach's, a Gardener; that they met Jackson and Carter, and told them what they had done and that they were going to get a Rope

and

and a Ladder, for Chater was not quite dead in the Well; that they all could not raise the Ladder; so they got some old Gate-Posts and Stones, and threw down upon him into the Well, and then left him.

The Prisoner Hammond desired the Witness might be asked, Whether, when they were at Old Mills's, he did not offer to ride away, and make a Discovery, but was prevented by the Company?

Raise said he never heard him say any Thing about it; but some of the Company, which he believed was Richards, did threaten any of the rest who should refuse to go to the Murder of Chater.

Ann Pescod, deposed, that two Men came to her Father's on the 15th of February, about one or two o'Clock in the Morning, and called for Thomas Pescod her Father; that she asked one of them his Name, and he said it was William Jackson: Her Father, who was then very ill, said they might come in if they would; that Jackson did come in, and asked if they could not bring a couple of Men with them to be there for a little while, to which she answered no, because her Father was ill; and thereupon Jackson turned to the other Man, and said, we cannot think of abiding here, as the Man is so ill, and so they went away. She saw that Jackson's Head was bloody.

She

She was ordered to look at the Prisoners Jackson and Carter, and see if they were the two Men that came, and she said Jackson was one; for that she took particular Notice of him, his Hand being bloody; and that she verily believed Carter was the other.

Then the King's Council call'd William Scardefield, who being sworn, deposed, that he kept the Red Lion at Rake, in the Parish of Rogate, and that in the Night, between the 14th and 15th of February last, the Prisoners Jackson and Carter, with Steele and Richards, came to his House, and call'd out to him, *For God's sake get up, and let us in*; then he let them in, and lighted a Candle, and saw they were bloody; he asked them how they came to be so? and they said they had an Engagement with some Officers, and had lost their Goods, and some of their Men they feared were dead, and some were wounded; that they said they would go and call them that were at the other Publick House; and while he was gone down into the Cellar, he heard Horses come to the Door; and some of the Men went into the Kitchen, some into the Brewhouse, and some into the Parlour; that he saw two or three Men in the Brewhouse, and there lay something like a Man before them in the Brewhouse, by the Brewhouse Door, and he heard them say he was dead; that some of them calling for Liquor, he carried a Glass of Gin into the Parlour,

lour, and saw a Man standing upright in the Parlour, with his Face bloody and one Eye swelled very much; that Richards was in the Parlour with the Man, and objected to his coming in, and the Prisoners Carter and Jackson, and three others were then in the Brewhouse, and Steel was with them; after they had drank three Mugs of Hot, they got their Horses out and sent him down for some Brandy and Rum, but when he came up with it, all the Company were gone 20 Yards below the House, though several of them came back to drink, one or two at a Time; that he did not know what became of the Man that he saw standing in the Parlour; but he observed they separated into two Companies; that one of the Company, a little Man, ask'd him if he did not know the Place where they laid up some Goods a Year and an half ago? and the Prisoner Carter came back, and said they must have a Lanthorn and Spade; that Richards fell in a Passion because he refused to go along with them, and upon seeing him coming towards them with a Light, the Company parted; that he saw a Horse stand at a little Distance, and there seemed to him to be a Man lying across the Horse, and two Men holding him on, and he believed that the Person he saw lying across the Horse was dead, but he was not nigh enough to see whether he was or not.

That when they came to the Place, one of the

[131]

the little Men began to dig a Hole; and it being a very cold Morning, he, the Witness, took hold of the Spade and help'd to dig; and in that Hole the Company buried the Body that lay cross the Horse.

That on the Wednesday or Thursday following, about twelve or One at Noon, the Prisoners Jackson and Carter, and all the rest of the Company, came again to his House; and the Prisoner Richard Mills the Younger, and his Brother John, were sent for, and came to them.

Edward Sones proved, that on the 16th or 17th of September last he found the Body of a dead Man in a Well in Harris's Wood, within 200 Yards of Lady Holt House, & that there were two Pieces of Timber over the Body; that he went immediately to get the Coroner's Inquest, and when he came back, he saw the Man had Boots on, and there was a Rope about his Neck; that the Well is by Lady Holt Park, in the County of Sussex.

Mr. Brackstone produced the Boots and a Belt that were taken off the Body, and given to him by the Coroner.

Mrs. Chater, the Widow of Daniel Chater, deposed, that she remembered her late Husband set out from Southampton on the 14th of February last, and that she had never seen him since that Time; she looked upon the Belt produced by Mr. Brackstone, and said she knew it was the same Belt her Husband had on when he set out from home, by a particular Mark in it; and she believed that the Boots produced were likewise her Husband's.

Mr. Sones proved also, that the Horse, which Chater sat out upon, was found about a Month afterwards and delivered to the Owner.

The King's Council submitted it here.

Mr. Justice Foster acquainted the Prisoners that the King's Council having gone through their Evidence, it was now Time to offer what they could in their own Defence.

He repeated to each of the Prisoners the particular Facts the Evidence had charged him with, and asked them severally what they had to say to clear themselves of that Charge.

To which the Prisoner Tapner said he did not know that they were going to murder the Man; but Jackson and Richards threatened to kill him if he would not go with them, and he received three or four Cuts from Hammond or Daniel Perrier, but he did not know which; that Richards and another Man tied the Rope; and he denied that he drew a Knife or cut Chater across the Face.

Mr. Justice Foster told him, that supposing he was threatened in the Manner he insisted on, yet that would be no legal Defence in the present Case; and that in every possible View of the Case, it was infinitely more eligible for

a

a Man to die by the Hands of Wicked Men, than to go to his Grave with the Guilt of innocent Blood on his own Head.

Cobby said he did not know what they were going to do with the Man, that he never touched him, and knew nothing of the Murder.

Hammond said, when he understood what they were going to do, he wanted to go off and make a Discovery; but the Company prevented him; and that by the Company he meant all the Prisoners.

Richard Mills the Elder, said he did not know what they were at, and did not think they would have hurt the Man; and did not know he was chained till after they were gone away.

Richard Mills the Younger, said he knew nothing of the Matter, and never saw either of the Men (Galley and Chater) in his Life; he acknowledged he was at Scardefield's House, but said he knew nothing of the Murder, and denied the Charge; that Scardefield was the only Witness he had, for he [Scardefield] knew when he came, and how long he staid there.

Jackson said, the Man who said he would be Chater's Butcher, was his Butcher, and nobody else, that he [Jackson] was not by when he was murdered, and was not guilty of it.

Mr. Justice Foster cautioned him not to deceive himself, and told him that with Re-

gard

gard to the present Charge, it was not necessary that he should have been present at the Murder; he was not charged with being present, but as an Accessary before the Fact, in advising and procuring the Murder to be done; and that was the Fact he was called upon to answer.

Carter said when he went to the Widow Paine's, he only thought they were going to carry the Men out of the Way, till they saw what should become of Dimar, and that he never laid Hands upon them. And went along with the Company to prevent Mischief.

Scardefield the Witness was then called again, and Richard Mills the Younger being asked whether he would ask him any Questions, only desired he might be asked what Time he came to his House, and how long he staid there; to which, Scardefield answered, that Mills came to his House about Half an Hour after one; staid there about an Hour and an Half, and went away on Foot.

The rest of the Prisoners said they had not any Witnesses.

Upon which, Mr. Justice Foster opened to the Jury the Substance of the Indictment as before set forth; and told them that whether the Prisoners or any of them were guilty in Manner as therein they are severally charged, must be left to their Consideration, upon the Evidence that had been laid before them.

That

That in order to enable them to apply the Evidence to the several Parts of the Charge, it would be proper for him first to acquaint them how the Law determines in Cases of this Nature; that with Regard to the Persons charged as Principals, wherever several Persons agree together to commit a Murder, or any other Felony, and the Murder or Felony is actually committed, every Person present aiding and abetting is, in the Eye of the Law, guilty in the same Degree, and liable to the same Punishment as he who actually committed the Fact. And the Reason the Law goes upon is this, that the Presence of the Accomplices gives Encouragement, Support, and Protection to the Person who actually commits the Fact: And at the same Time contributes to his Security.

That it is not necessary that the Proof of the Fact, in Cases of this Nature, should come up to the precise Form of the Indictment: For if the Indictment charges that A did the Fact, and that B and C were present aiding and abetting, if it be proved that B did the Fact, and that A and C were present aiding and abetting, they will be all guilty within the Indictment.

That Accessaries before the Fact, are those who not being present in any Sense of the Law at that Time the Fact is committed, have advised or otherwise procured the Fact to be done.

done. These Persons, in the Case of wilful Murder, will be liable to the same Punishment as those who committed the Murder, by their Instigation, Advice, or Procurement.

He then summed up the Evidence very largely, and applied it to the Case of the several Prisoners, and concluded, that if upon the whole, the Jury should be of Opinion that either of the Principals (Tapner, Cobby, Hammond, or the others charged as Principals in the Indictment) did strangle the Deceased, and that the Prisoners, Tapner, Cobby, and Hammond, were present aiding and abetting, they will be within this Imdictment.

And if they should be of Opinion, that the Prisoners, charged as Accessaries before the Fact, did advise, consent to, or procure the Murder, they likewise will be guilty within this Indictment, though they were not present when the Fact was committed.

The Jury, after some little Consideration, gave their Verdict, that Tapner, Cobby, and Hammond, were guilty of the Murder, as laid in the Indictment.

And
Richard Mills the Elder, Richard Mills the Younger, William Jackson, and William Carter, were guilty as Accessaries before the Fact. Chi-

[137]

Chichester, January 18th, 1748-9.

THE Judges came this Morning into Court between Nine and Ten o'Clock, and the Prisoners, who were convicted Yesterday, being brought from the Goal, they were all put to the Bar, but Cobby, Hammond, Tapner, and the Mills's were set aside, and Jackson and Carter set forward in order to be try'd for the Murder of William Galley.

Then the Clerk of the Arraigns bid William Jackson and William Carter to hold up their Hands, which they did, and he then read over to them the Indictment on which they had been arraigned the Day before, as Principals in the Murder of William Galley, and to which they had pleaded, Not Guilty.

Mr. Steele opened the Indictment to the Jury, and Mr. Bankes, the King's Counsel, spoke to much the same Purport as he had done the Day before.

Mr. Smythe, another of the King's Counsel, spoke as follows, viz. I shall only add a Word or two, to explain to you why these two Men, who were convicted Yesterday as Accessaries before the Fact to Murder of Chater, and thereby liable to suffer Death, should be tried a second Time, as Principals, for the Murder of Galley.

The Reasons for it are, in the first Place, it will be necessary to convict them as Principals for the Murder of Galley, otherwise, the

[138]

Accessaries to that Murder, either before or after the Fact, cannot be convicted.

Another Reason is, as the Intention of all Prosecutions, as well as Punishments, is not so much to revenge and punish what is past, as to deter others from committing the like Crimes, it may be of Service to the Publick to have every Circumstance of this cruel Transaction disclosed, to shew how dangerous to their Neighbours, and to the Country in general, those Persons are, who are concerned in Smuggling, and how much it concerns every Man to use his utmost Endeavours to suppress, and bring them to Justice; and it may have another good Effect, in preventing Persons from engaging in that lawless Practice, when they see it consequentially engages them in Crimes, which at first they might never intend; for I believe, if these unhappy Men had been told, when they first began Smuggling, that the Time would come when they would coolly bathe their Hands in the Blood of two innocent Men, (bad as they now are) they would then have been shocked, and startled at the very Imagination of it; yet Men are so naturally led from one Vice to another, that having once transgressed the Laws of their Country, they have insensibly arrived at such an Height of Wickedness, as to commit this heinous Crime without the least Hesitation or Remorse. After which the following Witnesses were called for the Crown, viz. Mr.

[139]

Mr. Milner, Mr. Sheerer, William Galley, Son of the Deceas'd, were severally produced and sworn, and Mr. Milner, Mr. Sheerer and William Galley gave the same Evidence as on the former Trial; as did Mr. Edward Holton of the Deceas'd, & Chater's calling on him at his House at Havant on Sunday the 14th of February, 1747-8.

Robert Jenkes also proved upon this Trial, the same as he did upon the former, with this Addition:

That when they were at the Widow Paine's, Jackson and Carter both said they would see the Letter for Justice Battine, because they thought the Men were going to swear against the Smugglers; that both Jackson and Carter hindered him from going through the Room where the two Men were; and that one of the Men had on a blue Great Coat.

Being cross-examined, at the Request of Carter, whether he hindered him from going through the Room?

Answered, That both the Prisoners did.

Joseph Southern, William Lamb, William Garret, and George Poate, proved the same, as upon the former Trial.

John Raiss, to the first Part of his Evidence relating to his Transactions at the Widow Paine's, added, that the Blood ran down from Galley's Head and Face, on Jackson's knocking him down; and that Galley and Chater were not fuddled when he went away.

Being

Being ask'd if he was certain the two Prisoners were present at Rowland's Castle, at the Consultation that was had to take the Men, Galley and Chater away and confine them, said, yes he was sure they were both present.

William Steele, to his former Evidence, added, That whilst they were at the Widow Paine's, Jackson said, " That if any of the " Gang went away from them, he would " shoot them through the Head, or through " the Body, or serve them as bad as the two " Men should be served." That he supposed Jackson meant by this, that he would murder any of their own Company, or use any of them as ill as they did the Officer and Chater, if they left them; that when the Company left off whipping Galley with their Thongs, and Lashes of their Whips, as mentioned in the former Trial, because the Lashes of the Whip reached this Witness, they beat him with the Butt-end of their Whips, which were very heavy, and loaded with Lead, till one of their Whips was beat all to Pieces; that the Gravelly Knap, where Galley was pushed off the Horse, when he died, was in Conduit-Lane, in Rogate Parish; and that Little Harry pushed him in the Back, and shoved him down; and that the Prisoners Jackson and Carter, Little Sam, and Richards, were in Company when he died; and that they laid his Body upon a Horse, and one Man held him on one Side, and another on the other Side,

and

and so they led the Horse along; that Carter and Jackson went before to call Scardefield up, and when they came there, they laid Galley's Body down in the Kitchen or Brewhouse at Scardefield's, and carried Chater into another Room; that they drank every one a Dram, and Jackson and Carter asked Scardefield if he knew any Place to bury that Man in, and he said no, but they said he must go with them; and they got a Spade, and a Candle and Lanthorn, and they laid Galley on Horseback again, and he (the Witness) Carter, Little Sam, and Scardefield, went back for about a Mile, and he held the Horse whilst Scardefield, Carter, & Little Sam, went to find the Place to bury him in; and when they had found it, Carter and Sam came back to him, and left Scardefield to dig the Grave; they went and buried him there, and returned back to Scardefield's again; that Jackson told them that whilst they were burying Galley, he and Little Harry went to carry Chater to Old Mills's; that they buried Galley two or three Feet deep, in the Heart of a Sand Pit, about three or four, or five o'Clock in the Morning.

Being cross-examined, and asked by Carter, whether he (Carter) struck Galley; answered, that they all struck him.

Being asked, at the Request of the Prisoner's Council, what was the Consequence of that Thrust which Little Harry gave Galley, when he fell the last Time? answered, That
he

he thought by the Fall Galley's Neck was broke, because as soon as he was down, he gave himself a Turn, and stretched out his Hands and Legs, and never stirred or spoke afterwards; that Galley was not falling, 'till Little Harry gave him the Push: Said he did not know the Parish of Rogate, or that the Place where Galley died was within that Parish, any otherwise than that he had been there since, and several People said it was the Parish of Rogate.

Mr. Staniford, who was Council for the Prisoners, moved, that the Place where Galley died was not in the County of Sussex, and therefore the Prisoners must be acquitted of this Indictment; for that the present Special Commission, by which their Lordships were trying the Prisoners, was only to enquire into Murders and Felonies committed in the County of Sussex.

Whereupon the Counsel for the King reply'd, that they would undertake to prove the Place in the County of Sussex; and for that purpose William Steele was then asked, whether the Gravelly Knap where Galley died was in the County of Southampton or County of Sussex? answered that he could not tell; that he had never heard, as he remembered, what County that Place was in, but he was carried thither last Friday, to see the Place, and he shewed to some People, then present, the Spot of Ground where Galley fell off

off the Horse, and died, and he believed he should know one of the Men that were with him.

John Astlett being called up, Steele said he was one of the Men that was there.

Astlett was then sworn, and proved that he was with Steele and some Dragoons on Friday last; that Steele pointed down to the Ground with a Stick, and said, "There the Man died:" That he (the Witness) took particular Notice of that Place, and is sure it was in the Parish of Harting in Sussex; that he now lives at Harting, and was born & bred just by, and had lived there ever since he was a Lad, & borne the Offices of Surveyor & Constable.

Steele being cross-examined, was ask'd how he could remember the Place again so as to be sure of it, said, He knew the Place very well again, by the little gravelly Rising of the Ground.

William Scardefield proved the same as in the former Trial, with the following Facts relating the Burial of Galley; that one of the Gang asked him if he knew the Place where they laid up some Goods about a Year and a Half ago, & he told them he did; upon which the Man said, "You must go along with us," but the Witness told him his Wife was ill, and he could not leave the House; and then Carter came in and asked for a Lanthorn, and Edmund Richards told him he must go with them, to which he replied, if he must go, go, he must; that when he came down the Hill a little Way from his own House, he saw two Companies, one on the Right and the other on the Left; that Carter, Steele, and a short Man he did not know, went on to the Place, and one of them came up after him, and told him where it was; upon which they brought the Horse up to a rough kind of a Dell, and the short Man fell a digging, and it being a very cold Night, he (the Witness) took the Spitter and dug to keep himself warm; there seemed to him to be a Man upon the Horse, and it fell into the Pit like a dead Man, and they covered it up; and he verily believed it to be the Body of a Man, but he did not help to put it in, and was about three or four Yards from it; he never went nigh the Ground afterwards, and did not see the Body of a Man upon the Horse afterwards, or any where else; that the Earth was thrown over the Pit, and the short Man did most of the Work; and he did not enquire, or chuse to ask any Questions about it.

Edward Sones proved the finding the Body of a dead Man, about the 15th of September, in a Fox Earth, within three Quarters of a Mile of Rake; that there were Boots upon the Legs, and a Glove upon one Hand; that the Body was very much perished, and had a Waistcoat and Breeches on.

John Greentree produced a Coat, which he took up beyond Harting Pond in the publick Road,

Road, on the 15th of February last, and swore that there were some Writings and a Letter Case in the Pocket, which he said he should know if he was to see them again.

Upon this a Parchment was delivered into Court by Justice Battine, a Justice of the Peace, in whose Custody it had been left (and shewn to the Witness) who said it was the same that he found in the Coat Pocket.

It was then read in Court, and appeared to be a Deputation under the Hands of the Commissioners of the Customs, dated the 1st of April, 1731, appointing William Galley to be a Tidesman in the Port of Southampton.

William Galley, Son of the Deceased, looked at the Coat which the other Witness produced, and proved it to be a Coat his Father had on on Sunday the 14th of February, 1747-8, when he set out with Daniel Chater for Major Battine's to carry a Letter to the Major.

John Greentree was call'd again, and said, that the Coat was very bloody when he found it.

The King's Council submitted it here, upon which the Prisoners being call'd upon to make their Defence,

The Prisoner Carter said he never intended to hurt the Man, and never struck him, and only intended to carry him away to take Care of him, till they knew what became of Dimar; and that he had not any Witnesses.

The Prisoner Jackson said little or nothing, only that he did not kill the Man, nor did not know who did.

The Prisoners having neither of them any Witnesses to produce, Mr. Justice Foster opened to the Jury the Substance of the Indictment, as before set forth, and told them, that where several People join to do an Act, in itself unlawful, and Death ensues from any Thing done in Prosecution of that unlawful Design, they will be all considered as Principals in Murder, if they were all present aiding or abetting therein; that it was not necessary that each of the Prisoners at the Bar should be guilty of every single Abuse that was offered to the Deceased, in the long Series of Barbarities the Witnesses for the Crown had laid before them ; if all or any of those Abuses contributed to his Death, and the Prisoners at the Bar were engaged in the several Designs against him, and present aiding and abetting the others, they will be guilty within this Indictment.

He summed up the Evidence very largely, and applied it to the Case of the Prisoners; and then left it to the Consideration of the Gentleman of the Jury.

The

The Jury after some little Consultation together, gave their Verdict, that William Jackson and William Carter were both Guilty.

The Council for the Crown then mov'd for Judgment; and all the seven Prisoners being set to the Bar, and severally asked what they had to say why Judgment of Death should not pass on them, Old Mills said, he had nothing to say, only that he knew nothing of the Murder of Chater.

Young Mills said he was not at Scardefield's a Quarter of an Hour; and that it was by Accident he called there, and that he knew nothing of the Murder.

Hammond and Cobby said, they were compell'd to stay by Richards and Jackson, and that they would have made their Escapes but could get no Opportunity to do so.

Tapner said, he did not cut Chater cross the Face, neither could he tell who did.

Jackson and Carter said, that they had nothing more to say than what they had already said.

And none of the Prisoners or their Counsel having any Thing to offer in Arrest of Judgment, Mr Justice Foster spoke to them as follows:

Benjamin Tapner, John Cobby, John Hammond, William Jackson, William Carter, Richard

chard Mills the elder, and Richard Mills the younger, you have been convicted upon very full and satisfactory Evidence of the Murder of Daniel Chater ; three of you as Principals, and the Rest as Accessaries before the Fact.

And you William Jackson and William Carter stand farther convicted, as Principals in the Murder of William Galley.

Deliberate Murder is most justly rank'd amongst the highest Crimes human Nature is capable of ; but those you have respectively been convicted of, have been attended with Circumstances of very high and uncommon Aggravation.

The Persons who have been the Ojects of your Fury, were travelling on a very laudable Design, the Advancement of publick Justice. For this they were beset in their Inn, tempted to drink to Excess, and than laid asleep in an inner Room, while a Consultation was held in what Manner to dispose of them ; and in the End a Resolution was taken to carry them to some distant Place, and to dispatch them by some Means or other.

In Consequence of this Resolution they were set on Horseback, and exercised with various Kinds of Cruelty for many Hours together, 'till one of them sunk under the Hardships he suffered, and died upon the Road.

The other was carry'd to a Place of safe Custody, there kept chain'd on a Heap of Turf,

Turf, expecting his Doom for three Days. During this dreadful Interval, a second Consultation was held, and a Resolution taken to dispatch him too; not a single Man, of thirteen who were present, offering one Word in his Behalf.

He was accordingly hurry'd to his Death; and though he begged earnestly to live but one Day longer, that small Respite was deny'd him. I will not repeat every Circumstance; but I cannot forbear putting you in Mind of one. When the poor Man was told he must die that very Night, some of you advised him to say his Prayers, and accordingly he did address himself to Prayer.

One would have hop'd that this Circumstance should have softened your Hearts, and turned you from the evil Purpose you were bent upon. Happy had it been for you, if you had then reflected, that God Almighty was witness to every Thing that pass'd among you, and to all the Intentions of your Hearts!

But while the Man, under great Distraction of Thought, was recommending his Soul to Mercy, he was interrupted in his Devotion by two of you, in a Manner I scarce know how to repeat.

I hope your Hearts have been long since softened to a proper Degree of Contrition for these Things; and that you have already made a due Preparation for the Sentence I am now to pass upon you.

If

If you have not, pray lose not one Moment more. Let not Company, or the Habit of Drinking, or the Hopes of Life divert you from it ; for Christian Charity obliges me to tell you, that your Time in this World will be very short.

Nothing now remains but that I pass that Sentence upon you which the Law of your Country, in Conformity to the Law of God, and to the Practice of all Ages and Nations, has already pronounced upon the Crime you have been guilty of. This Court doth therefore award that you Benjamin Tapner, William Carter, John Hammond, John Cobby, Richard Mills the Elder, Richard Mills the Younger, and William Jackson, and each of you shall be conveyed from hence to the Prison from whence you came, and from thence you shall be led to the Place of Execution, where you shall be severally hanged by the Neck, until you shall be dead, and the Lord have Mercy upon your Souls.

Having now compleated the Trials of these seven bloody Criminals, I shall next give you the short Appendix which has been publish'd by three of the Clergymen who attended them after their Conviction, and who have signed their Names to the same : After which I shall give

[151]

give a much fuller Account of their wicked Lives and Behaviour.

After Sentence the Prisoners were carried back to Chichester Jail. The Court were pleas'd to order them all for Execution the very next Day, and that the Bodies of Jackson, Carter, Tapner, Cobby, and Hammond, the five Principals, should be hung in Chains. Accordingly they were carried from the Jail to a Place call'd the Broile near Chichester; where, in the Presence of great Numbers of Spectators on Thursday the 19th Day of January last, about Two o'Clock in the Afternoon, all of them were executed, except Jackson, who died in Jail, about four Hours after Sentence of Death was pronounced upon him.

The Heinousness of the Crimes of so notorious Offenders may possibly excite in the Reader a Desire to be informed of their respective Behaviour, whilst under Sentence of Death, and at the Place of Execution; to satisfy which is subjoined the following authentick Account, under the Hands of the several Clergymen who attended them alternately in Jail, and together at the Place of Execution.

" The first Time I went to the Malefactors
" under Condemnation, being the Evening
" after Sentence was passed upon them, I pray-
" ed with them all; viz. Carter, Tapner, Gob-
" by, Hammond, and the two Mills's (Jackson
being

[152]

"being dead just before I went to the Jail) but many Persons being present I had no Opportunity of saying any thing material, and therefore told them I would visit them early the next Morning, which I did accordingly.

"After Prayers, I talked with them about their unhappy Condition, and the heinous Crimes that brought them into it. I asked them, if they desired to receive the Sacrament, they all and each of them begged that I would administer it to them; accordingly I attended them again, about 10 o'Clock, for that Purpose; and during the whole Time of my performing that Office, they all behaved with great Decency and Devotion, especially Carter and Tapner.

"Afterwards I put the following Questions to them, and desired they would be sincere in their Answers as dying Men; first, Whether they did not acknowledge the Sentence that was passed upon them to be just, and what they highly deserved? Carter, the most sensible and penitent amongst them, first answered, Yes; as did afterwards Tapner, Cobby, and Hammond; but the two Mills's did not.

"2dly, I asked them whether they forgave every Body? They all and each answered, they forgave all the World. Tapner then owned, that Edmund Richards and another

"were

" were the Cause of his Ruin, but yet forgave
" them.
" Carter laid his Ruin to Jackson, for
" drawing him from his honest Employment.
JOHN SMYTH,
Curate of St. Pancrass, in Chichester.

" Both Carter and Tapner, a few Hours
" before their Execution, confess'd to me,
" that they, with several others, assembled
" together, with a Design to rescue Dimar
" out of Chichester Goal; that the only Per-
" son amongst them, who had Arms, was
" Edmund Richards; but that being disap-
" pointed by a Number of Persons, who had
" promised to join them from the East, their
" Scheme was frustrated, and their Purpose
" carried no farther into Execution; that one
" * Stringer was at the Head of this Con-
" fedracy, but not present with them at
" the Time of their assembling together.
"
SIMON HUGHS,
Vicar of Donnington, in Sussex.

" Benjamin Tapner of West Stoke in Sussex,
" Labourer, Son of Henry Tapner of Alding-
" borne, in Sussex, Bricklayer, aged 27, before
" he was turned off, owned the Justice of his
Sentence,

* This Stringer is Thomas Stringer, who stands indicted as a Principal in the Murder of Daniel Chater, but is not yet taken.

[154]

"Sentence, and desired all young Persons to
"take Warning by his untimely End and
"avoid bad Company, which was his Ruin.
"When in Goal, before he was brought out
"for Execution, he said, he did not remem-
"ber he put the Rope about Chater's Neck.

"William Carter of Rowland's Castle, in
"Hampshire, Thatcher, Son of Wm. Carter
"of East Meon in Hants, Thatcher, aged 39,
"both at the Place of Execution and in the
"Gaol, confest the Justice of the Sentence
"passed upon him, and in both Places acted
"more suitably to a Person in such unhappy
"Circumstances than any of them: He
"likewise at the Gallows, in the same Man-
"ner as Tapner did, cautioned every one a-
"gainst those Courses that had brought him
"to so shameful an End. Tapner and Carter,
"when all the Ropes were fixed, shook
"Hands, but what, or whether any Words
"then passed between them, was not heard.

"Richard Mills the Elder, of Trotten, in
"Sussex, Colt-breaker, Son of ——— Mills of
"Liss, in Hants, Labourer, aged 63, was un-
"willing to own himself guilty of the Fact
"for which he died, and said, he never saw
"Chater; but being ask'd whether he never
"heard him, as he was confined so long, and
"in so terrible a Condition, in the next Room
"to that in which he generally sat, made no
"Answer.

Richard

" Richard Mills the Younger, of Stedham,
" Sussex, Colt-breaker, Son of the aforesaid
" Richard Mills, aged 37, would willingly
" have been thought innocent; and it being
" put to him, whether he made that Speech
" about the Council of War, &c. and whe-
" ther he was not at the Consultation? denied
" both; but in the latter, Tapner confronted
" him, and said, yes young Major, you was
" there;" to which Mills replied, " ay, for a
" Quarter of an Hour, or so, or to that Pur-
" pose." It so happened that his Rope was
" first fixed to the Gallows, and a considerale
" Space of Time was taken up in fixing the
" rest; which Interim he might have much
" better employed, than he did, in gazing one
" while at the Spectators, and then at the
" Hangman (who was on the Gallows, tying
" the Ropes of the other Malefactors) till the
" Cart was almost ready to drive away.

" John Cobby of Sidlesham, in Sussex, La-
" bourer, Son of James Cobby, of Birdham, in
" Sussex, Carpenter, aged 30, appeared to be
" very dejected, and said but little in Jail, and
" little at the Gallows.

" John Hammond of Bersted, in Sussex, La-
" bourer, Son of John Hammond of the same
" Place, Labourer, aged 40, seemed likewise
" very much dejected, and had little to say for
" himself, excepting his pretending that the
" Threats of Jackson, Carter, and the rest,

" were the Occasion of his being concerned
" in the Murder.

" Cobby's Excuse was much the same.

" They all, except the two Mills's, seem'd
" sensible of the heinous Nature of the Crime,
" for which they died, and behaved as became
" Men in their unhappy Condition, more
" particularly Carter; but the Mills's, Father
" and Son, appeared hardened and unaffect-
" ed, both in the Jail and at the Gallows;
" especially the Son, appeared hardened and
" most insensible, and seemed by his Beha-
" viour, which has been mentioned before,
" even when his Rope was fixed to the Gal-
" lows, to be as little moved at what he was
" about to suffer, as the most unconcerned
" Spectator. However, just before the Cart
" drove away, he and his Father seemed to
" offer up some Prayers to God.

R. SANDHAM,
Vicar of Subdeanry in Chichester.

JOHNS MYTH,
Curate of St. Pancrass.

As Jackson died so soon after Condemnation, no other Account can be given of him,
than that he was of Welsworth, near Rowland's
Castle in Hampshire, Labourer, aged about 5o
Years; and that being very ill, all the Time
of his Trial, as he had been for a considerable Time before, was shocked at the Sentence
of Death, and the Apprehensions of being
hung

[157]

hung in Chains, to such a Degree, as hastened and brought on his Death, before he could pay the Forfeit of his Life, in that Ignominy, to which he was most deservedly doomed, and more particularly due to him as a Ringleader in the most cruel and horrid Barbarities and Murders.

He professed the Romish Religion some Years before his Death, and that he died a Roman Catholick may very reasonably be presumed from a printed Paper which was found carefully sewed up in a Linnen Purse in his Waistcoat Pocket, immediately after his Death, supposed to be a Popish Relique, and containing the following Words, viz.

Sancti tres Reges
Gaspar, Melchior, Balthasar,
Orate pro Nobis nunc et in Hora
Mortis Nostræ.
Ces Billets ont touché aux trois Testes de
S. S. Roys,
A Cologne. Ils sont pour Des Voyagers,
contre
Les Mal-Heurs de Chemins, Maux de Teste, Mal-caduque, fievres, Sorcellerie, toute forte de Malefice. Morte subite.

In English thus:

Ye Three Holy Kings
Gaspar, Melchior, Balthasar,

Pray

Pray for us now, and in the Hour of Death.

These Papers have touch'd the three Heads of the Holy Kings at Cologne.

They are to preserve Travellers from Accidents on the Road, Head Achs, Falling Sickness, Fevers, Witchcraft, all Kinds of Mischief, and sudden Death.

The Body of William Carter was hung in Chains, in the Portsmouth Road, near Rake in Sussex; the Body of Benjamin Tapner on Rook's Hill, near Chichester; and the Bodies of John Cobby and John Hammond upon the Sea Coast, near a Place called Selsey Bill, in Sussex, where they are seen at a great Distance, both East and West.

The Bodies of the Mills's, Father and Son, having neither Friend or Relation to take them away, were thrown into an Hole, dug for that Purpose, very near the Gallows, into which was likewise thrown the Body of Jackson. Just by is now erected a Stone, having the following Inscription, viz.

Near this Place was buried the Body of William Jackson, a proscribed Smuggler, who upon a special Commission of Oyer and Terminer, held at Chichester, on the 16th Day of January, 1748-9, was, with William Carter, attainted for the Murder of William Galley, a Custom-house Officer; and who likewise was, together with Benjamin Tapner,

[159]
Tapner, John Cobby, John Hammond, Richard Mills, the Elder, and Richard Mills, the Younger, his Son, attainted for the Mur-Murder of Daniel Chater ; but dying in a few Hours after Sentence of Death was pronounced upon him, he thereby escap'd the Punishment which the Heinousness of his complicated Crimes deserved, and which was the next Day most justly inflicted upon his Accomplices.

As a Memorial to Posterity, and a Warning to this and succeeding Generations.

This Stones is erected
A. D. 1749.

Having now given the Account of the Behaviour of these seven bloody Criminals, as occurred to the three Clergyman, who attended them after their receiving Sentence of Death, and who signed their Names to the same ; we shall now insert the Account of their Behaviour, from the Time of their being brought to Chichester Gaol, to their Execution, which Account was taken by two Persons who constantly attended on them, and is what occurred at the Times the Clergymen before-mention'd were not present ; and are inserted to make this Account compleat.

The

The seven Prisoners that were condemn'd, together with William Combleach the Gardener, committed on Suspicion of being concern'd in the Murder of Daniel Chater, were brought from Horsham Gaol in one Waggon, under a strong Guard of Soldiers, to Chichester, on Friday the 13th of January, 1748-9.

Jackson being sick, was kept up Stairs in a Room by himself; and the other seven, William Combleach being with them, were put in a lower Room, all iron'd and stapled down, and well guarded; but behav'd very bold and resolute, and not so decently as became People in their Circumstances. They eat their Breakfast, Dinner, and Supper, regularly, without any seeming Concern, and talked and behav'd freely to every Body that came to see them. Old Mills looking out of a Window the Day after they came there, which was Market-Day, young Mills said to Tapner, D--n the old Fellow, he will have a Stare out.

I. Richard Mills, sen. was formerly very well respected by the Gentlemen of the County; but having had for many Years Concerns with the Smugglers, and a Smuggler himself, and having prevail'd on his Sons, whom he had brought up to his own Business, to go a Smuggling likewise, he lost most of his Business and Character. He frequently said, that he was only sorry for his Sons, for as to himself, he was under no Trouble, for he was sure that he could not, according to the common

mon Course of Nature, live above a Year or two longer.

A few Hours after Sentence was pass'd upon him, a Clergyman who liv'd near him, went to see him in the Gaol, in order to discourse with him, and bring him to a true Sense of his deplorable Condition; to which Purpose he recommended to him to make use of his few remaining Moments in preparing for Eternity. While the Clergyman was thus seriously talking to him about the Concerns of his Soul, the Old Man interrupted him, and said, When do you think we shall be hang'd? The Gentleman after reproving him for the little Concern he discover'd about the more important Affairs of another World, told him he believ'd his Time was very short, and that he thought his Execution would be ordered some time the next Day, but could not exactly say at what Hour. Mills replied, that as to the Murder it gave him but little Trouble, since he was not guilty of it: But as to the Charge of Smuggling, he own'd he had been concern'd in that Trade for a great many Years, and did not think there was any Harm in it.

Being particularly ask'd, if he did not know that Chater was kept chain'd in his Turf-House; he answered very indifferently, That he could not tell, he believed he did, but what was that to the Murder? But being told that his Maid Ann Bridges had declar'd

upon

upon Oath, That he got up when Jackson and Little Harry * brought Chater to his House about Three o'Clock in the Morning, & that he order'd her not to go into the Turf-House, for there was a Person there whom it was not proper she should see; he could not tell what to say, but stood seemingly dumb-founded; and an Answer being press'd from him, he acknowledged, That he did get up, and let them in, and told Little Harry to carry him, Chater, into the Turf-House, and chain him; and that he, as well as Little Harry, did look after him till the Gang came and took him away the Wednesday Night, but that he was no Ways concern'd in the Murder; but at last he did acknowledge, That he did know they had agreed to carry Chater to the Well by Lady-Holt Park, and hang him, and throw him into it; and that Tapner took a Cord for that Purpose from his House.

Old Mills had been poor some Time, and had left off Smuggling, that is, going with the Gangs to the Sea-side to fetch the Goods being sensible of the Danger of going with others

---

* Little Harry is Henry Sheerman, who was condemn'd at the last Assizes at East Grinsted for the County of Sussex, for the Murder of Galley; and stood also indicted for the Murder of Chater, but was try'd only on the first Indictment. He was executed at Rake, near where Galley was bury'd, and there hung in Chains. An Account of him at his Trial, under Condemnation, and at the Place of Execution, will be inserted in the following Numbers.

[163]

others in a Gang with Fire-Arms; but he got something by letting the Smugglers bring any Thing to his House; and to blind the Neighbours, he liv'd privately with his Maid Ann Bridges, and had, for upwards of a Year, receiv'd Alms from the Parish, as he himself acknowledged.

2. Richard Mills jun. had been concerned in Smuggling for many Years. He was a daring, obstinate, hardened Fellow, and seemed capable of any Mischief. He said to a Gentlemen who went to see him in Gaol, that he did not value Death, but was not guilty of the Murder of which he was accus'd, since he was not present when it was done; though if he had, he should not have thought it any Crime to destroy such informing Rogues. After his Trial was over on Tuesday, two Gentlemen going up to see him, they told him that his Brother John * who had been advertis'd in the Gazette as an Accomplice in the Murder of one Hawkins, by throwing him into Parham Pond, and was likewise concerned in the Murder of Mr. Chater, but not then taken, was seen following the Judges over Hynd Heath, in their Way

---

* This John Mills is the same Person as went by the Name of Smoaker, who was condemn'd at the last Assizes at East Grinstead, for the County of Sussex, for the cruel Murder of Richard Hawkins, and is hung in Chains near the Dog and Partridge on Slendon Common; and whose Trial follows this Account of the seven condemned at Chichester.

Way to Chichester; What, said Mills, there has been no Robbery committed upon the Highway lately has there? Upon which the Person reply'd, Not that he had heard of. Mills made Answer, I suppose Jack must take to the Highway, for he has no other Way to live, till an Opportunity offers of his getting over to France, which I heartily wish he may do. After their Conviction of Tuesday Night for the Murder of Chater, he and the rest of them were remanded back to Prison, and order'd to be brought down the next Day, when Jackson and Carter were to be tried for the Murder of Galley, and the Whole to receive Judgment; when Mills said, What the D————l do they mean by that? Cou'd not they do our whole Business this Night, without obliging us to come again and wear out our Shoes. Well! if it must be so, the Old Man and I will go first, but I will give the Old Man the Wall, as he accordingly did.

3. John Cobby, seem'd a harmless, inoffensive Creature, and being of an easy Temper, it is suppos'd, he was the more easily influenc'd to take on with the Smugglers, tho' he declar'd he had not long been with them. He acknowledg'd that he was at the Well when Chater was hung, and flung into it, and that he, as well as the rest, were all guilty of the Crime for which they were condemn'd. He was very serious, and seem'd very penitent; own'd he was a great Sinner; begg'd Pardon

of

of GOD for his Offences, and hop'd the World would forgive him the Injuries he had done to any body.

4. Benjamin Tapner, was born of very honest Parents, who gave him good Schooling; and he always lived in good Repute, till being persuaded by Jackson, and some others who had been old Smugglers, to follow their wicked Courses; which he had done something more than two Years. He behaved all the Time, under his Confinement, more decently than some of the others, and frequently pray'd very devoutly. He was always very reserv'd if mention was made of the Cruelties he exercised on the deceased Daniel Chater. A Gentleman who desires his Name may not be mentioned, went to see him on Tuesday Evening, just after his Conviction, who taking him to one Corner of the Room they were all confin'd in, ask'd him, if there was any thing in the Report of his picking Chater's Eyes out? when he declared as a dying Man, he never made use of any Weapon but his Knife and Whip; and that he might in the Hurry pick one of his Eyes out with the Point of his Knife, for he did not know what he did, the Devil had got so strong Hold of him. He said, he had been in many Engagements with the King's Officers, and been wounded three Times; and hop'd all young People would take Warning by his untimely
Fate

Fate, and keep good Company, for it was bad Company had been his Ruin.

5. William Carter, behaved himself very serious, and said, that Jackson had drawn him away from his honest Employment many Years ago, to go a Smuggling, which was the Cause of his Ruin; and that they had been as sworn Brothers in Smuggling; and indeed his general Character was very good, except in that Particular. He declared that these Murders would never have happened, had not Mrs. Paine at Rowland's Castle sent for him and Jackson, and in some Measure exasperated them against Galley and Chater, as being informers. This Mrs. Paine and her two Sons are in Custody in Winchester Gaol, in order to take their Trials at the ensuing Assizes, when it is hoped they will meet their just Reward.

6. John Hammond, was a harden'd obdurate Fellow, and very resolute, and always held great Antipathy against the King's Officers, or others concern'd in suppressing Smuggling; and often would let drop Words out of his Mouth, as that he did not think it any Crime in killing an Informer; but when he came to receive Sentence he began to cry very much. He frequently relented for the Case of his poor Wife and four Children, and said, that was all that touched him; as for dying he did not mind it.

7. William

[167]

7. William Jackson died in his Room about 7 o'Clock the same Night he had received Sentence of Death. He had been one of the most notorious Smugglers living in his Time; and most of them, as well as Carter, gave him the worst of Characters, and that he was even a Thief among themselves; for when he knew that any of them had got any Run Goods, he would contrive some Way or other to steal them away from 'em. He reflected on himself, after receiving Sentence, for what he had said on his Defence at his Trial, about Ben Tapner, in saying Tapner only was guilty; for he declared they were all concerned; and that when he had been concerned in the Murder of Galley, he contriv'd to bring Cobby, Hammond, the three Mill's, Stringer, Tapner, and the rest of the Gang in to be concerned in the Murder of Chater, that least they might one Day or other, run to the Government, and make themselves an Evidence, as they might have done, but by being guilty of Murder, it would be an entire Bar to any of them.

The Afternoon preceding their Execution, a Person came to the Prison to take Measure of Jackson, Cobby, Hammond, Carter, & Tapner, in order to make their Irons in which they were to be hung in Chains; which threw the Prisoners into very great Disorder and Confusion, and they seem'd under a greater Concern than ever they had shew'd before. But when

when Old Mills and his Son were told that they were exempted from that Part of the Punishment, they seem'd to be mightily pleased at it, and contented to be hung only as common Malefactors.

But it deserves particular Notice, with respect to Jackson, that he was no sooner told that he was to be hung in Chains, but he was seiz'd with such Horror and Confusion, that he died in two Hours afterwards; and tho' he was very ill before, yet it is believ'd that this hastened his End, and was the immediate Cause of his Death.

The foregoing Accounts are a melancholy Proof of the dreadful Effects, which are the fatal but too frequent Consequences of the Offence of Smuggling; a Crime, which however prejudicial to the Kingdom in general, and to every fair Trader in particular, perhaps may not, from an Inattention to the many and monstrous Mischiefs deriv'd from it, have met with that general Detestation and Abhorrence it so highly deserves.

But a Perusal of these Sheets, shocking to every Reader, cannot fail to alarm the Nation, and open the Eyes of all People, who must reflect with Horror upon a Set of dissolute and desperate Wretches, united by a Parity of Inclinations and Iniquites, form'd into dangerous Gangs and Confederacies, that, encouraged by Numbers, they might exercise Cruelties, and common Barbarities, which, a-
bandoned

bandon'd as they were, they singly durst not attempt. Villains! not to be won by Lenity, despising and rejecting proffered Pardons, proceeding from Crime to Crime, till they arriv'd at the highest, and, until now, unheard of Pitch of Wickedness: Who, not content with defrauding the King in his Customs and Revenues; not satisfy'd with violating the Properties and Possessions, pursued the Lives of his Subjects and Servants, whose very Blood could not satiate their Malice;—— Tortures were added to aggravate the Pangs of Death.

Before we take Leave of these Wretches, and begin upon the Account of that most notorious Villain and Murderer John Mills, and the rest, as promised, we think it will be very necessary to inform our Readers of their several Behaviours at the Place of Execution, not mentioned before in the Account given by the three Clergymen.

At the Place of E X E C U T I O N.

THEY were brought out of the Gaol about Two in the Afternoon of Thursday the 19th of January, 1748-9, being the Day after their receiving Sentence, when a Company of Foot-Guards, and a Party of the Dragoons who lay in Chichester, were drawn out ready to receive them, and to conduct them

them with Safety to the Place of Execution, which was about a Mile out of Town. The Procession was solemn and slow; and when they came to the Tree, they all, except the two Mills's, behav'd a little more serious than they had done before. Cobby and Hammond said very little; acknowledged they had been Smugglers, which had brought them to this untimely End; and laid the Blame entirely on Jackson, who not only was the Person that persuaded them to turn Smugglers, but also was the Person who came to them, and persuaded them to go to Old Mills's, where Chater was.

Carter said, the Sentence was just on them all, for they were all guilty, as charg'd in the Indictments; and lamented the Case of his Wife and Children, and said, he hoped others would take Warning by his untimely End.

The Mills's, as I observ'd before, seemed no Ways concerned; and the young one said, he did not value to die, for he was prepared, tho' at the same Time appeared so very hardened and abandoned. The Halter that was for the Old Man was full short, the Gallows being high; so that he was obliged to stand a Tiptoe to give room for it to be tyed up to the Tree; the old Fellow saying several Times while this was doing, Don't hang me by Inches.

Tapner

[171]

Tapner appeared very sensible of his Crime, and prayed aloud, and seemed, as I hope he was, very sincere and devout. He declared, that Jackson, Cobby, and Stringer held three Pistols to his Head, and swore they would shoot him if he did not go and assist in the Murder of Chater, the Old Shoemaker, who was going to make an Information against their Shepherd Dymer, alias Diamond; that they also extorted 3 Guineas from him by the same Way of Threats, to repay Jackson and Carter what they had been out of Pocket on that Account. He said they were all guilty of the Crimes laid to their Charge; and that one T——ff, well-known in Chichester, & Stringer, * John Mills, and Richards, all not taken, were as guilty as himself; and as they deserved the same Punishment, he hop'd they would all be taken, and serv'd the same he was just going to be. He acknowledged cutting the Man cross the Face, but did not care to repeat any of the Cruelties he had exercised

We are now come to a Conclusion of the Trials, and the Behaviour of those that were executed at Chichester, and shall next proceed to

---

* This is the John Mills, since executed and hung in Chains on Slendon Common, Sussex, for the Murder of Richard Hawkins; and of whom we shall give a particular Account.

to those that were brought on at the Assizes at East Grinstead, where two of the same Gang were tried for Murder; namely Sheerman for that of Galley, & John Mills, called Smoaker, for that of Hawkins, who was destroyed in as cruel and barbarous a Manner as either Galley or Chater. After which we shall give an Account of the Trials of the other Smugglers which were very remarkable for the most notorious Crimes with which they are charged, such as Murder, House-breaking, Robberies on the Highway, &c. But as Sheerman was try'd for the Crime for which several others had been already convicted, as has been before related, we think his Trial will most properly follow those of his Confederates, and with whom he had been concerned throughout the whole Course of their Villanies: After which will follow the Trial of John Mills, otherwise Smoaker, who not only had a Hand in the Murder of Chater, but likewise was a Principal in that of poor Hawkins, and the Ringleader of all these barbarous Scenes of Cruelty.

Henry Sheerman, otherwise Little Harry, was indicted for the inhuman Murder of William Galley, which the said Sheerman, in Company with several others did perpetrate and accomplish on the said William Galley, by tying and fastening him on a Horse, and then lashing, whipping, and beating him with their Whips, till the said Galley, no longer able to bear

[173]

bear the cruel Scourges, fell with his Head under the Horse's Belly, and his Feet across the Saddle; that being again set upright on the Horse, the said Prisoner, with the rest, again whipp'd, beat, and bruised him, by the Means of which he fell of the second Time, and being set on another Horse, the said Prisoner with the others again beat and whipp'd him, till the said Galley was so terribly bruised and wounded, that being ready to fall off the Horse, the Prisoner gave him a Push, and threw him to the Ground, of which Blows, Wounds, Bruises, and Fall from he said Horse, he died.

The Council for the King upon this Indictment were the same as were upon that against John Mills and John Reynolds, who after laying open and explaining to the Court and Jury the heinous Nature of the Offence, and the pernicious Consequences of Smuggling, which generally brought on Murder, Robbery, and other enormous Crimes, they produced the following Witnesses, in Support of the Charge against the Prisoner.

Mr. Sheerer, Collector of the Customs at Southampton, depos'd, that he receiv'd a Letter from the Commissioners of the Customs, informing him, that one John Dimar was taken up on Suspicion of being concern'd with others in breaking open the Custom-house at Pool, and committed to Chichester Goal; that thereupon he sent one Chater with a Letter to Justice Battine, under the Care of the deceased William

William Galley, the 14th Day of February was Twelvemonth, and hired a grey Horse for him to ride on.

William Galley, the Son of the deceased William Galley, depos'd, that he very well remembered, that some Time in February was Twelvemonth, his Father set out on a Journey to Justice Battine; that the Night before he went he saw the Letter, and saw the Direction upon it, which his Father was carrying to the Justice; that his Father was dress'd in a blue Great Coat, lined with blue, with Brass Buttons, a light brown close-bodied Coat, trimmed with blue, his Waistcoat and Breeches the same, and rode upon a grey Horse, and that he never saw his Father afterwards.

George Austin depos'd, That on the 14th of February was Twelvemonth, being at the New Inn at Leigh, he saw the deceased William Galley, and another Person on Horseback, and hearing them enquire the Way to East Marden, and shewing a Letter they had for Justice Battine, he said, that he and his Brother Thomas Austin, and his Brother-in-Law Robert Jenkes, were going Part of that Road, and would shew them the Way; that he went with them to a Place called Rowland's Castle, to a publick House kept by one Widow Paine; that being there, Galley and his Companion call'd for Rum. That the Widow Paine enquired of him if he was acquainted

quainted with those Men, or whether they belonged to his Company. He told her they were going to Justice Battine's; upon which she apprehended there was something in Hand against the Smugglers, several of whom came in soon afterwards.

John Rase, otherwise Raise, an Accomplice in the Fact, being sworn, depos'd, that on the 14th of February was Twelvemonth, he was at Rowland's Castle about the Middle of the Day; that when he came in he saw there Edmund Richards, William Steel, Carter, Jackson, Little Sam, Richard Kelly, Jackson's Wife, and the Prisoner Henry Sheerman, together with Galley and Chater; that he saw Jackson take Chater to the Door, and heard him ask him whether he knew any thing of Dimar the Shepherd, and Chater answering, that he was oblig'd to appear against him, Galley came to them, to interrupt their talking, which Jackson resenting, struck him on the Face with his Fist. Being all come into the House again, Jackson related to the rest of them, what Chater had said in relation to Dimar; upon which they consulted together what to do with Galley and Chater, and it was agreed by them all to carry them to a Place of Security, till they should have an Opportunity of sending them to France; and that the Prisoner was present at this Consultation.

William Steele, another of the Accomplices in the Fact, from Beginning to the End, being

being sworn, depos'd, that on the 14th of February was Twelvemonth, he was sent for to the Widow Paine's; that when he came there he found Jackson, Little Sam, Kelly, Carter, Richards, Raise, and the Prisoner Little Harry; that he saw the two Strangers there, Galley and Chater, who were drinking with the Prisoner, and the rest of the Smuglers; that Jackson took Chater out of the House, and was followed by Galley, who soon after returned with his Face bloody, having, he said, been knock'd down by Jackson. That Galley and Chater wanting to be gone, the Prisoner, with the rest of the Smugglers, persuaded them to stay, and the Company continued drinking till Galley and Chater were quite drunk, and were led into a little inner Room to sleep; this was about four or five o'Clock. That in the mean while this Witness, with the rest of the Smugglers, the Prisoner being present, consulted what to do with Galley and Chater; and it was propos'd to make away with them, and to that End, to throw them into the Well in the Horse Pasture, about a Quarter of a Mile from Rowland's Castle; but upon second Thoughts that Well was judged too near, and might occasion a Discovery. That then it was agreed to allow Three-pence a Week each, and to keep them in some private Place, till they saw what was the Fate of Dimar; and as Dimar was used, in the same Manner they agreed to use Galley and Chater.

That

That about Seven o'Clock Carter and Jackson went into the little Room, and having waked Galley & Chater, brought them out all bloody, and believed that Jackson and Carter had kick'd them with their Spurs, which they had just before put on; that they then brought Galley and Chater out to the Street Door, and set them both upon the same Horse, and tied their Legs together under the Horse's Belly. That then he (this Witness) got upon a grey Horse, and led that the deceased and Chater were upon; that they had not gone above 80 Yards, before Jackson call'd out, Whip the Dogs, cut them, slash them, damn them; and then the Company fell to lashing and whipping them with their Horsewhips, while they rode about a Mile to a Place call'd Wood's Ashes; that there they all alighted, and the Prisoner, Little Harry, gave each of them a Dram, but none to Galley and Chater; that mounting their Horses again, they fell to beating and lashing the two Men as violently as they had done before, till they came to Dean, which was about Half a Mile farther; that then one of the Company pulled out a Pistol, and swore he would shoot them (Galley and Chater) through the Head, if they made any Noise, while they were passing through that Village; when they were got through Dean, they fell to whipping them again, till they came almost to Idsworth, when Galley and Chater fell again with their Heads under the

A a   Horse's

Horse's Belly; upon which they parted them, and set up Galley behind him, this Witness, and Chater behind Little Sam, and thus proceeded towards Lady-Holt-Park, about three Miles further, whipping them all the Way; but the Lashes of their Whips falling on this Witness, he cried out, and they left off whipping Galley; That being come to Lady-Holt-Park, Galley being faint and tired, got off, and Jackson and Carter took him by the Arms and Legs, and carried him to a Well there, into which they said they would throw him; but some of the Company interposing, they set him up behind this Witness, and went on till they came down a Hill, and Galley not being able to ride any further, got down again; upon which they laid him upon the Pummel of the Saddle, across a Horse before Richards, with his Belly downwards, and in this Manner carried him about a Mile and a Half; that then Richards being tired of holding him, let him down by the Side of the Horse; that then they put him upon the grey Horse which this Witness rode upon, and this Witness got off; they sat him up, his Legs across the Saddle, and his Body lay over the Mane, and Jackson held him on, and went on in this Manner for about Half a Mile Galley crying out grievously all the Time, Barbarous Usage! Barbarous Usage! For God's sake shoot me thro' the Head, or thro' the Body; he (the Witness) imagined that Jackson was squeezing his privy Parts.

That

That they went on for two Miles farther, and coming to a dirty Lane, Carter and Jackson rode forwards, and bid them stop at the Swing Gate beyond the Water till they return'd. Being gone a little while, they came back again, and said, that the Man of the House where they had been, was ill, and could not entertain them. It was then propos'd to go to the House of one Scardefield at Rake; upon which the Prisoner tied Galley with a Cord, and got up on Horseback behind him, in order to hold him on; and coming to a Gravelly Knap on the Road, Galley cried out, I shall fall, I shall fall; whereupon the Prisoner then said, D———n you, then fall, and gave him a Push, and Galley fell down, gave a Spirt, and never spoke afterwards; he (the Witness) believed his Neck was broke by the Fall; that then they laid him across the Horse again, and went to the Red Lion at Rake, kept by William Scardefield, whither they carried Chater all over bloody. That Jackson and the Prisoner went from Scardefield's, with Chater, to Old Mills's, where he was left to the Care of the Prisoner; and in the mean Time they buried Galley.

This Witness was ask'd by the Court, whether the Prisoner was present at the first Consultation at the Widow Paine's, and continued in the same Company to the Death of Galley, and he answered, yes, he was with them all the Time.

[180]

Then William Scardefield was sworn, who depos'd, that the Prisoner at the Bar was with the rest of the Smugglers, at his House at Rake, when Galley was brought dead there; but went away with Chater, the other Man, who was all bloody.

The Council for the King said, they had a great many more Witnesses, but they would rest the Matter as it now was, and not give the Court any further Trouble.

The Prisoner being called upon to make his Defence, said, he had no-body to disprove the Facts, or speak to his Character; and said, he was sent for to Rowland's Castle, tho' he did not know for what; that when he came there, he was threatened by Jackson, Richards, and others that were there, that they would shoot him thro' the Head, if he would not go with and assist them in what they were going about, and that it was not in his Power to make his Escape from them.

The Jury brought him in Guilty. Death.

Having now given the Trial of Henry Sheerman, alias Little Harry, at East Grinstead, it will be necessary next to give an Account of his Life, and Behaviour under Sentence of Death, and at the Place of Execution, before we proceed to the Trial of that notorious Villain John Mills, alias Smoaker, for the cruel Murder of Richard Hawkins.

Henry Sheerman, alias Little Harry, about 32 Years

Years of Age, was born and bred up at West-Strutton in the County of Sussex, to Husbandry, whose Parents were People of good Character, tho' of but middling Circumstances; and gave him as good an Education at School as they could afford; but he said, he never minded his Learning, his Mind run more upon other Things, so that he made but a very little Progress, tho' he could read very well, and write a little.

He said, that Jackson was the Cause of his Ruin, and the considerable Gains that were allowed to those who were as Servants to the Master Smugglers, seduced him to leave his honest Employment, and take on with them.

He often declared, that he never was concerned in any other Murder than that of Galley, for which he suffer'd; but being asked, if he was not guilty of the other Indictment that was against him, as being an Accessary to the Murder of Chater before the Fact was committed, he evaded answering the Question in full, and said, he left the Company and Chater, and did not go to the Well where he was hanged, and flung down; but on his being interrogated very much, and informed it was the same Thing, his knowing their Intention of murdering Chater, tho' he did not go quite to the Place, he said, he did keep him chain'd in Old Mills's Turf-House, and that he did know that the Company, when he parted from them, were going to hang him in the Well

at

at Lady-Holt-Park, and then to fling his Body down it, to prevent a Discovery. He was ask'd, if old Major Mills knew that Chater was confin'd in his Turf-house, and that they were going to murder him, because old Mills partly denied it when he was executed on the Broyl near Chichesther; he said, that old Mills was guilty of the whole Affair laid to his Charge, as being concern'd in the Murder of Chater; that old Mills gave him the Chain and Horse-Lock, to chain Chater to the Beam in his Turf-House, and went frequently to see he was safe during his Confinement there, and often told Chater, that he was a Villain to turn Informer, and he would see he should be hang'd, to prevent his informing any more; and he declar'd, that when they took Chater from old Mills's House, that old Mills knew that they were going to hang him at the Well by Lady-Holt-Park, and that the Resolution and Agreement of him, old Mills, as well as the rest, was to fling his Body down there, it being a dry Well, to prevent a Discovery; and that old Mills himself said, That it was a very proper Place for Concealment, for as it was a dry Well, it might lie there an Age before any Thing could be discover'd; and before that Time it would be rotted quite away to nothing.

Before we proceed any further we shall inform the Reader what Encouragement is given to seduce the young People from their honest
Em-

Employments to turn Smugglers, which Little Harry declared.

The Master Smugglers contract for the Goods either abroad, or with the Master of a Cutter that fetches them, for a Quantity of Teas, (which they call Dry Goods), and Brandies, and the Master of the Cutter fixes a Time and Place where he designs to land, and seldom or ever fails being pretty punctual as to Time, especially if the Weather permits; as the Master Smugglers cannot fetch all the Goods themselves, so they hire Men whom they call their Riders; and they allow each Man Half a Guinea a Journey, and bear all Expences of eating and drinking and Horse, and an Allowance of a Dollop of Tea, which is 40 Pound Weight, being the Half of a Bag, the Profit of which Dollop, even of the most ordinary Sort, is worth more than a Guinea, and some Sorts 25s. and some more; and they always make one Journey, some times two, and sometimes three in a Week, which is indeed such a Temptation that very few People in the Country could withstand; and which has been the Cause of so many turning Smugglers.

He said it was very hard Work in going down to the Sea-side to fetch the Goods, and considering the Hazard they run if taken, and of their own Persons, as they are obliged to ride of Nights only, and thro' all the by-Ways, avoiding all the Publick Roads as much

[184]

much as possible, People would not take on with them if it were not for the great Profits that arise.

He said that all the Smugglers both Masters and Riders drink Drams to great Excess, and generally kept themselves half drunk; which was the only Thing that occasioned them to commit such Outrages as they did sometimes; and he gave the following Account of the Murders of Galley and Chater.

That on Sunday the 14th of last February was 12 Months, he was sent for to the Widow Payne's, and inform'd that there were two Men there, who were going to make an Information against John Dymer, who they call'd their Shepherd, that was in Custody at Chichester, on Suspicion of being concern'd in breaking open the King's Warehouse at Poole; that, as he was one concern'd in the said Fact, he readily went to hear what he could, and when he came there he found Jackson, Richards, Steele, the Evidence, and some more of the Gang concerned in breaking open the said Warehouse at Poole, when Jackson said to him, Harry, I have sent for you, here are two Men have got a Letter to Justice Battine, for him to take an Information against the Shepherd; and that (they the Smugglers) resolved to have the Letter from them; which he among the rest agreed to; and after they had made the Men drunk, Carter and Kelly went into the Room where the Men were put to Sleep, and

[185]
and took the Letter out of one of their Pockets, which they read, and found the Contents amounted to all they suspected; that it was never proposed by any of the Men to hurt either Galley or Chater, but to keep them privately to prevent their giving the designed Information, till the Women, Carter's and Jackson's Wives, proposed hanging them; and then it was talk'd of carrying them to the Well just by, and to hang them and fling them down it, but it was not agreed to; neither did any of the Men in his Presence or hearing shew or intimate any Inclination towards their so doing.

He said further, that they all drank pretty freely to make Galley and Chater drunk, and then when they came to the Resolution of carrying them both away, and concealing them till they knew what would be the Fate of the Shepherd Dymer, they were all more than half drunk; that he verily believ'd none of them had any Design of murdering them while they were at Rowland's Castle; but Jackson, who was the drunkest of the Company call'd out to whip them, which was soon after they set out from Mrs. Payne's House, when Edmund Richards, who is not yet taken, began to lash them with his long Whip; and then they all did the same except Steele, who was leading the Horse the two Men rode on.

He said that the Design of tying their Legs under the Horse's Belly was for no other Reason

son than to prevent their jumping off and running away, and making their Escape, as it was Night time; which if either of them should do, they would be all inevitably ruined.

The Liquor they had drunk, and giving way to their Passion, urged them on to the Cruelties they exercised on Chater; but when they found Galley was dead, it sober'd them all very much, and they were all in a great Consternation and Surpize, and could not tell what to do, when they concluded to bury the Body of Galley, and to take Care of Chater. [Here he related the Affair of Jackson and him carrying Chater to Old Mills's, all of which has been related fully before.]

He lamented the unhappy Case of Chater during the Time of his being chained in Old Mills's Turf-house, but said, Self-preservation obliged him to take Care he did not get away, tho' he was all the Time very uneasy; and said he declar'd his Abhorrence to Tapner's cutting him cross the Face and Eyes, and of Cobby's kicking him while he was saying the Lord's Prayer, and that he came out of the Turf-House into the Dwelling-House upon that Account, not being able to bear hearing the poor Man's Expressions in begging for a few Hours or Minutes to make his Peace with his Creator, at the same Time the Blood running all down his Face. He said it was not Cobby alone that kick'd Chater while he was

was at Prayers, but also Richards and Stringer, who are both not yet taken.

Being asked, why he did not give the poor unhappy Men, Galley and Chater, a Dram, as well as the Smugglers, when they all got off their Horses, when they had whipped the Men about Half a Mile ? said, he was going to do it, but Richards, Carter, and Jackson, all three swore they would blow his Brains out if he did.

He acknowledged going away with them all, from Old Mills's House, in order to hang Chater, according to the Agreement; but that seeing Tapner whip the poor Man so cruelly, as they went along, Chater at the same Time being all over Blood and Wounds, his Heart relented, and that was the only Reason why he did not go all the Way with them, and be present at his Murder.

At his Trial he behaved with a seeming Reservedness, but no way audacious, as some of the others were; and after he had received his Sentence, which was the Day after he was tried, he began to bemoan his unhappy Circumstances, and prayed very devoutly; and confessed, that he had been a very wicked Liver ever since he turned Smuggler.

He said, he never was concerned in many Robberies, as Numbers of the Smugglers had been; and what gave him the most Uneasiness was, the great Scandal and Vexation he had brought on his Wife and Family.

He was convey'd under a strong Guard of Soldiers from Horsham to Rake, near the Place where Galley was buried, on the 2oth Day of March, 1749, and there executed, and afterwards hung in Chains, as an Example.

At the Place of Execution he behav'd very penitent, and as became one in his unhappy Circumstances, frequently saying that Jackson was the original Person who was the Cause of his Ruin; and that he should not have gone to the Widow Payne's, that unfortunate Day that Mr. Galley and Mr. Chater were there, had he not been sent for. He declar'd, that at the Time he gave Galley the Push off the Horse, when Galley fell down and died, he had no Thought that that Fall would kill him just then; that he begg'd Pardon of GOD and Man, not only for that wicked Action of his Life, but for all others; and then was turn'd off, crying to the Lord JESUS CHRIST to receive his Soul.

We shall now proceed to the Trials of John Mills, alias Smoaker, and John Reynolds, the Master of the Dog and Partridge on Slendon Common, where Richard Hawkins was inhumanly murder'd; and then give an Accout of John Mills's wicked Life, and Behaviour at his Trial, and under Sentence of Death; and also of his Confession, and last Dying Words at the Place of Execution.

John

[189]

John Mills, alias Smoaker, (together with Jeremiah Curtis, alias Butler, alias Pollard, and Richard Rowland, alias Robb, both not yet taken,) was indicted for the Murder of Richard Hawkins, in the Parish of Slendon, in the County of Sussex, on the 28th Day of Jan. 1748-9, in the 21st Year of his Majesty's Reign, by violently assaulting, sticking, beating, whipping and kicking him the said Richard Hawkins over the Face, Head, Arms, Belly and private Parts; of which Wounds, Bruises, Kicks and Stripes he instantly died. And John Reynolds was indicted for aiding, assisting, comforting and abetting the said John Mills alias Smoaker; and Jeremiah Curtis, alias Butler, alias Pollard, and Richard Rowland, alias Robb, both not yet taken in the Murder of the said Richard Hawkins.

The Council for the King were Mr. Staples, Mr. Steele, Recorder of Chichester, Mr. Burrell, Mr Symthe, one of the King's Council learned in the Law, and Member of Parliament for East-Grinsted, in the County of Sussex, and Mr. Serjeant Wynn.

One of the Council for the King having opened the Indictment, Mr. Symthe observed to the Court and Jury, That the Practice of Smuggling having prevailed all over the Kingdom, particularly in that and the neighbouring Counties, to so great a Degree, and the Persons concerned therein become so very audacious, that a great many Murders were
com-

committed, and very barbarous ones too, upon such Persons who should shew the least Inclination to prevent their pernicious Practices. That the Murder for wnich the present Prisoners were indicted, was one of the most bloody, and most cruel that ever was perpetrated in this, or any other civilized Nation, excepting two others that had happened in this County. That the Prisoner Mills seemed to have the Honour of committing the first, and setting the Example of this Species of most terrible Murders, though some Persons who committed the other Murder, had been first brought to Justice. That many People were induced to think Smuggling was no Crime at all, or if it was one, but a very small one; it was but cheating the King, and that was no Harm; not at all considering that it is a Crime not only against the Laws of the Land, but against the Law of God also which commands all Men to render to Cæsar the Things that are Cæsar's. That Smuggling was robbing the Nation of that Revenue which is appointed for Payment of the National Debt; and that every Act of Smuggling was defrauding every one of his Majesty's Subjects that pay Taxes, as they are obliged to make good all Deficiencies. That when they shall hear the Witnesses, they will find that this evil Practice was the original Cause of this Murder, and then he did

not

not doubt but they would find the Prisoners guilty.

Mr. Serjeant Wynn, after speaking of the Nature of the Crime, and that it was one of the consequential Evils that attended Smuggling, observed further, That most of the most daring Robberies and Insults that had been lately committed, were by these Sort of Men, who thought, or at least acted as if they thought themselves above all Law. That when they had called their Witnesses, he did not doubt but they would give the Jury such satisfactory Evidence as would induce them to believe the Prisoners guilty, and consequently find them so.

Henry Murril deposed, That some Time in January last was Twelvemonth, he was informed, that some Persons were at his House, enquiring after some Tea they had lost, but could not tell who they were; that he went to young Cockrel's, who keeps a Public House at Yapton; there he saw Jerry Curtis, and two others, drinking; Curtis was very angry, said, some Rogues had stole two Bags of Tea from him, and d——n him, he would find it out, and severely punish those concerned therein; for, d——n him, he had whipt many a Rogue, & wash'd his Hands in their Blood: That Curtis had offered this Deponent five Guineas to get the Tea again, or find out who had got it; and then said, that if Money could not get it,

he

he would come Sword in Hand and find it out, and take it away.

Being ask'd by the Court, if the Prisoner Mills was one of them that were with Curtis? said, he could not tell.

Henry Titcomb deposed, That one Day in January last was Twelvemonth, Curtis and Mills came to Mr. Boniface's Barn, where he, the Prisoner, and Richard Hawkins the deceased were at work; that Curtis called Hawkins out to speak with him; that he did not hear what passed between them, but that Hawkins went away with them; that a little while after, the same afternoon, he saw Hawkins riding behind Mills from Warburton towards Slendon, and never saw Hawkins the deceased afterwards.

John Saxby deposed, that he was a Servant to Cockrel the Elder of Warburton; that the Day Hawkins the deceased was missing, Curtis, Mills, and Hawkins came to his Master's House, and drank together; that at going away, Mills bid Hawkins get up behind him, which he at first refused, saying, he would not, without making a sure Bargain; that they bid him get up, for they would satisfy him, which Hawkins did; and this Deponent never saw the Deceased afterwards.

Thomas Winter, alias the Coachman, an Accomplice, deposed, That one Day the latter End of January was Twelvemonth, he, with Jerry Curtis, alias Pollard, were at the Prisoner

soner Reynold's House, who kept the Dog and Partridge on Slendon Common ; that Curtis presently went away from him, and promised to come to him again very soon, for he was to pay this Witness some Money he owed him ; that this Deponent staid at the Dog and Partridge the rest of the Day ; that towards Evening, Richard Rowland, alias Robb, came to the House, ask'd for his Master Curtis, & staid with this Deponent till Night, when the Prisoner Mills and Curtis came; that Curtis called for Robb, & said, Robb, we have got a Prisoner here ; then Hawkins got down from behind Mills, and all went in together to a Parlour in the Prisoner Reynolds's House; that they ordered a Fire to be made, and call'd for Liquor; that they all, viz. Hawkins the deceased, Curtis, Mills, Rowland, otherwise Robb, and this Deponent, sat down together ; that then they began to examine Hawkins about the two Bags of Tea, which he denied, saying, he knew nothing of the Matter ; that Curtis said, Damn him, he did know, and if he would not confess, he would whip him till he did, for damn him, he had whipt many a Rogue, and wash'd his Hands in his Blood : That the Prisoner Reynolds came in when they were urging the deceased to confess, and said to the Deceased, Dick, you had better confess, it will be better for you; his Answer was, I know nothing of it. After Reynolds was gone, Mills and Robb were very angry with the Deceas'd; that Robb struck him in the Face, and made his Nose bleed, and threaten'd to whip him to Death; that Mills shew'd that he was pleas'd with what Robb had done, and again threaten'd the Deceased, who said, If you whip me to Death I know nothing of it. That then Mills and Robb made the Deceased strip to his Shirt, then they began to whip him over the Head, Face, Arms and Body, till they were out of Breath, he all the while crying out, that he was innocent, and begg'd for God's sake, and Christ's sake, to spare his Life for the sake of his Wife and Child: That when they were out of Breath, they pull'd off their Cloaths to their Shirts, and whipp'd him again till he fell down; when he was down, they whipp'd him over the Legs and Belly, and upon the Deceased's kicking up his Legs to save his Belly, they saw his private Parts; then they took Aim thereat, and whipp'd him so, that he roar'd out most grievously; that then they kick'd him, over the private Parts and Belly; they in the Intervals asking after the Tea, the Deceased mention'd his Father and Brother, meaning the two Cockrels that upon this Curtis and Mills took their Horses, and said they would go and fetch them, and rode away, leaving the Deceased with Robb and this Deponent. That after they were gone, he and Robb placed the Deceased in a Chair by the Fire, where he died.

Being

John Mills alias *Smoaker*, & *Rich^d, Rowland* alias *Robb*, Whipping *Rich^d, Hawkins*, to Death, at y^e *Dog & Par--tridge on Slendon Common*; & *Jeremiah Curtis*, & *Thos. Winter* alias *Coachman*, Standing by Aiding & abetting ye Murder of the said *Richd Hawkins.*

Being asked by the Court, if the Deceased was in good Health when he came to the Prisoner Reynolds's House, and if he believ'd he died of the ill Usage he there met with? His Answer was, He was in good Health when he came there, and was a stout Man, and was sure he died of the Kicks and Bruises he received from Mills and Robb.

He further deposed, that when they found he was dead, Robb locked the Door, put the Key in his Pocket, then they took their Horses, and rode towards Warburton to meet Curtis and Mills; that in the Lane leading to Warburton he met them, with each a Man behind him; that he desiring to speak with them, the Men behind them got off, and stood at a Distance. That this Deponent asked Curtis what they were going to do with those two Men? Who answered, to confront them with Hawkins; then the Deponent told him he was dead, and desired no more Mischief might be done; when Curtis replyed, By G——d, we will go through with it now. That this Deponent begged that the two Men might be sent home, for there had been Mischief enough done already; that then Curtis bid the two Men go home, and said, when they wanted them they would fetch them. That they rode all together to the Prisoner Reynolds's House, when Reynolds said to Curtis, You have ruined me; and Curtis reply'd he would make him Amends. That then they consulted ed what to do with the Body, when it was proposed to throw him into a Well in Mr. Kemp's Park, and give out that they had carried him to France ; that the Prisoner Reynolds objected to it, as that was too near, and would soon be found. That they laid him on a Horse, and carried him to Parham Park, about 12 Miles from Slendon Common, where they tied large Stones to him, in order to sink the Body, and threw him into a Pond belonging to Sir Cecil Bishop.

John Cockrel the Younger, deposed, That the 28th of January last was Twelvemonth, about Ten o'Clock at Night, the Prisoner Mills came to his House, called for some Ale, ordered his Horse into the Stable ; that while he was in the Stable, Curtis came in, and demanded two Bags of Tea, which he said, his Brother-in-Law had confess'd he had got ; that this Deponent denied his having them, upon which Curtis beat him with an Oake Stick till he was tired ; that after this they took him with them to his Father's at Warburton, where they took his Father and him with them, to carry them to Slendon, on Mills's and Curtis's Horses, one behind each, and about a Mile before they came to Slendon, they met two Men on Horseback, who call'd to them, and said they wanted to speak with them ; that then they were order'd to get off from behind Curtis and Mills ; that after the two Men had talk'd with Curtis and Mills

some

some Time, Curtis bid them go Home, and when they wanted them, they would fetch them.

John Cockrel the Elder being sworn, confirm'd his Sons's Evidence, as to their being carried away, and dismiss'd by Curtis.

Being ask'd by the Court, how long after his Son-in-Law the Deceas'd was missing, it was before he heard his Body was found, said, that in the April following he was sent for to Sir Cecil Bishop's, that there he saw the Deceas'd Richard Hawkins in a most terrible mangled manner, having a Hole in his Skull, that he knew him by the Finger next his little Finger of his Right-Hand being bent down to his Hand.

Matthew Smith depos'd, That one Night in January last was Twelvemonth, he was at the Prisoner Reynolds's House, the Dog and Partridge on Slendon Common, and saw Curtis and Mills ride up to the Door, (Mills with a Man behind him) and Curtis call'd out to Robb, and said, We have got a Prisoner; and that then they all went in together into the back Parlour.

Richard Seagrave, another Witness, depos'd, That he liv'd at Sir Cecil Bishop's in Parham Park, and saw the Body of a Man taken out of a Pond there, very much mangled and bruis'd, and was likewise present when John Cockrel the Elder came there, and said he knew the

the Body to be his Son-in-Law's, Richard Hawkins.

Jacob Pring, another Witness, depos'd That being at Bristol, he there fell in Company with the Prisoner Mills; that they came together from thence to his House at Beckingham in Kent; that on the Road he ask'd him, whether he knew of the Murder of Richard Hawkins of Yapton; that he told him, Yes, and related to him the particular Manner in which it was done, as follows, that in the Beginning of January was Twelvemonth, they had two Bags of Tea stole from the Place where they had conceal'd some Stuff, and suspecting Hawkins and the Cockrels to have it, he and Jerry Curtis went and fetch'd Hawkins from a Barn where he was at work, and carried him to Reynolds's on Slendon Common, where Robb and Winter, commonly call'd the Coachman, were before them; that he and Robb whipp'd Hawkins with their Horse-whips, till he own'd that the Cockrels had their Tea; that then he and Curtis went and fetch'd the Cockrels, and as they were bringing them behind them on the Road, Robb and Winter met them, and told them, that the Man was dead whom they had whipp'd; that they then sent the Cockrels home, and went and took Hawkins's dead Body, and carried it to Parham Park, and threw it into Sir Cecil Bishop's Pond.

Here

[199]

Here the Council for the King rested it.

The Prisoner being called upon to make his Defence, denied the Murder, and said he left the Deceased Richard Hawkins alive and well with Robb and Winter, when he and Curtis went to fetch the Cockrels, and how Hawkins came by his Death he could not tell. This was Mills's Defence.

The Council for the Prisoner Reynolds, objected to the Indictment, and said, tho' it might be extreamly right with regard to the Prisoner Mills, yet it was not so with regard to the Prisoner Reynolds; for as Reynolds was indicted as a Principal in the second Degree, he should be concluded in the Judgment as all Principals are in Murder. The Court said, That this was Matter that might be offered in Arrest of Judgment, but not at that Time.

The Council in his Defence said, That the Prisoner Reynolds was no ways privy to or concerned in the said Murder; that the Persons who brought Hawkins to his House were in a Room by themselves, and what they did there was without the Privity or Knowledge of the Prisoner Reynolds, and that they should call Witnesses to prove the same.

William Bullmar was called, who deposed, that one Day in January last was Twelvemonth, he was at the Prisoner Reynolds's House with William Rowe in the Kitchen; that he saw Curtis in the House, and heard there

there were other People with him in the new Back-Parlour : that himself was there till Twelve o'Clock at Night, and that the Prisoner Reynolds was with him during all that Time, excepting when he went to draw Beer for his Customers in the Kitchen.

William Rowe deposed, that he was at the Prisoner Reynolds's House at the same Time as the before-mentioned Witness, that he saw Curtis and Mills in the House, and heard there were other People with them, in the Back-room; that he staid till Twelve o'Clock at Night, during which Time the Prisoner Reynolds was with him in the Kitchen, except when he was called upon to draw Drink for the Company in the Kitchen.

The Judge, after he had summed up all the Evidence exactly in the Manner it had been sworn, observed to the Jury, that with regard to the Prisoner Mills, the Facts were proved extreamly clear, as he had called no Witness to contradict the Evidence in any Shape, for the King; that with respect to the Prisoner Reynolds, it did not appear that he was in the Party that committed the Murder, but that he was at home at Peace in his own House, when this Transaction happened; if therefore, they believed the Witnesses called on his Behalf, they must acquit him, and the Jury, without going out, found Mills

[201]

Mills guilty, Death. And acquitted Reynolds *.

Mills's Behaviour was very unbecoming one under his Circumstances; but before we proceed to say any Thing more of this Criminal, we will give the Particulars of his being apprehended. The 31st of January last a Proclamation was issued for the apprehending several notorious Smugglers that were concern'd in the Murder of Richard Hawkins of Yapton, naming this John Mills as one of them; promising his Majesty's Pardon to any one who should apprehend or give Information of any of the Offenders, altho' such Informer was an out-law'd Smuggler, provided he was not concern'd in any Murder, or in breaking open his Majesty's Ware-house at Poole. Now William Pring, who was a Witness against the said Mills and the two Kemps, knowing himself to be an out-law'd Smuggler, yet not concern'd in Murder, nor in breaking open the Ware-house at Poole, resolves if possible to get his own Pardon, by taking some of those Offenders. To this Purpose he apply'd to a

* N.B. Notwithstanding James Reynolds was acquitted of the Murder, yet as it appeared very plain, that he concealed the Murder, by knowing the same had been committed by the Prisoner, and the others, who stand Indicted for the same; as being present at the Consultation of concealing the Murder, and of burying the dead Body, and advising therein, and his Wife also being present, they were both Indicted for the same, and are to be try'd at the next Assizes.

D　　　　　　Great

Great Man in Power, informing him, that he knew Mills, and that if he could be asssured of his own Pardon, he would endeavour to take him, for he was pretty certain to find him either at Bristol or Bath, where he knew he was gone to sell some Run Goods. Being assur'd of his Pardon, he set out accordingly, and at Bristol unexpectedly found the two Kemps with him, whom he likewise knew, as being notorious Smugglers. They then began to talk together about their Affairs. Mills was in a Proclamation for two Murders, that of Chater and that of Hawkins; Thomas Kemp was advertised for breaking out of Newgate, and Lawrence Kemp was out-lawed by Proclamation, and both the Kemps were concerned in robbing one Farmer Havendon.

After talking over Matters together, and observing that all their Cases were very desperate Pring, as a Friend, offered his Advice, by which he intended to inveigle them into the Snare he had laid for them. He said, since they were all alike in such desperate Circumstances, without any Hopes of mending their Condition, he would have them go with him towards London, and to his House at Beckingham in Kent, and there consult together, to go and rob upon the Highway, and break open Houses in the same Manner as Gregory's Gang used to do. Upon which they all agreed to come away together; and upon the Road, amongst other Talk, Mills own'd that he was
one

one of those who committed the Murder of Hawkins, and both the Kemps confess'd that they were concerned in robbing Farmer Havendon, in the Manner it was proved upon their Trials.

When they were all come to his House at Beckingham, Pring then pretended, that his Horse being a very indifferent one, he would go to Town and fetch his Mare, which was a very good one, and would come back again with all convenient Speed, and then they would set out together upon their intended Expeditions; for as their Horses were very good, and his but a bad one, it might bring him into Danger, in Case of a Pursuit. Upon which he set out, and they agreed to stay at his House till his Return; but instead of going to Town, he rode away to Horsham, where he applied to Mr. Rackster, an Officer in the Excise there; who, together with seven or eight more, all well armed, set out for Beckingham, in order to take them, where they arrived in the Dead of Night, and found Mills, and the two Kemps just going to Supper upon a fine Breast of Veal, and secured them. They bound the Arms of the two Kemps, but Mills refusing to be bound in that Manner, and being very refractory, they were forced to cut him with one of their Hangers, before he would submit. They then brought them all three to the County Gaol for Surry, where they found Robert Fuller & Jockey Brown in

Custody for Smuggling; and knowing that they had been guilty of many Robberies on the Highway in Sussex, they applied to the Government for a Habeas Corpus, to carry them all five down to the Assizes at East Grinsted, where though they were each try'd only upon one Indictment, yet there was another Indictment for Murder, besides two for Robberies against Mills, another for a Robbery against Fuller, and two other Indictments against the two Kemps, besides a Number of other Prosecutors, who were ready at East Grinsted to lay Indictments against them, if there had been Occasion.

John Mills, about 30 Years of Age, Son of Richard Mills, of Trotton, lately executed at Chichester, was bred up to the Business of a Colt Breaker by his Father. He said he had been a Smuggler many Years, and blamed Jeremiah Curtis, alias Pollard, who stands indicted for the same Murder he was convicted of, and William Jackson, who was condemn'd at Chichester, for the Murders of Galley and Chater, as being the principal Persons concern'd in drawing him away from his honest Employment.

Young Mills acknowledged himself a very wicked Liver; but complained of the Witnesses, that is, such of them as had been Smugglers, and turn'd Evidences, and said that they had acted contrary to the solemn Oaths and Engagements they had made and sworn

sworn to among themselves, and therefore wish'd they might all come to the same End, and be hang'd like him, and d——n'd afterwards.

John Mills stood Indicted for two Murders, besides Robberies, as is before mention'd; but it is remarkable that he commited both Murders in 20 Days; that of Hawkins, for which he was condemned, was perpetrated on the 28th of January; and the other, that he was not try'd for, which was the Murder of Daniel Chater, he commited the 17th of the following Month.

It having been said, as soon as Mills was convicted, that the Design of him and Curtis in fetching the two Cockrels, the Father and Brother-in-Law of Hawkins, to the Dog and Partridge, was to serve them as they had done Hawkins; Mills being ask'd the Question, at first seemed very sulky; but at last said, he believed that if Winter and Robb had not met them, and told them Hawkins was dead, they should have basted the Cockrels well, when they had got them there; so that in all Probability their Lives were preserv'd, by Hawkins's dying sooner than his Murderers expected.

Jeremiah Curtis, alias Pollard, is at Graveline in France, and has enter'd himself into the Corpse of the Irish Brigades; but Richard Rowland, alias Robb, he imagined, for very good Reasons, was not out of the Kingdom; and

[206]

and indeed he was seen and spoke to on East-Grinsted Common, which is near that Town, the latter End of the Month of January last.

Being ask'd if he was upon Hind Heath on Saturday the 14th of January last, when the Judges were going over it to hold the Assizes at Chichester on the Special Commission, to try his Father and Brother, and the rest of the Smugglers then in Custody, for the Murders of William Galley and Daniel Chater; he said he was, and two others were with him, but would not tell their Names; that they had no Manner of Design against the Judges, or any body with them, neither did he or his Companions know or think of the Judges coming at that Time, for they were upon other Business; and that he and his two said Companions committed three Robberies that Afternoon and Evening, the nearest being upwards of 12 Miles from Hind Heath; but he refused to name any Particulars, declaring he thought he merited Damnation if he was to discover any Thing, by Means of which any of his Companions might be apprehended and convicted.

At the Place of * Execution he behaved himself much more sedate than he had done before,

* He was executed on a Gibbet, erected on Purpose, on Slendon Common, near the Dog and Partridge, and afterwards hung in Chains on the same Gibbet.

before, during the small Time he lay under Condemnation, and prayed very devoutly; as he did indeed all the Way from the Gaol to the Place of Execution, to which he was conveyed under a strong Guard of Soldiers. He owned the Fact of the Murder of Richard Hawkins for which he suffered; but said when he went away with Curtis to fetch the two Cockrels, he did not think the Man was so near his Death.

He likewise acknowledged being present at the Consultation at Scaredefield's, when it was agreed to Murder Daniel Chater, the Shoemaker, who was at that Time confined in his Father's Skilling or Turf-House; and also that he was concerned with the two Kemps in going with Crapes over their Faces, and robbing Farmer Havendon, of Heathfield, in the County of Sussex.

He was press'd hard to make an ingenious Confession of all the Crimes he had been guilty of, but he refused; and said any thing that was known to the World already, he would inform them how far he was concerned in them, but nothing else.

Being then asked if he was with the Gang when the King's Custom-house at Poole in Dorsetshire was broke upon, he said he was, for it was too well known to deny it.

Just before he was turned off, he declar'd he was sorry for his ill spent Life, and desired all young People to take Warning by his untimely

[208]

timely End; and said that Richard Rowland, alias Robb, was only a Servant to Curtis, and was ordered by Curtis to assist him in whipping poor Hawkins; for the Cruelties of which and the Murder of Chater, and all other wicked Actions of his Life, he hoped God would forgive him; declaring he died in Peace with all Mankind, and therefore hoped for Forgiveness.

We will next proceed, and give the Trials, in a concise Manner, of Jocky Brown, the two Kemps, Fuller and Savage, all Smugglers, and tried at the same Assizes at East-Grinsted, in Sussex, and then proceed, and give an Account of their wicked Lives and Conversations; And first, we shall proceed on the Trial of Jocky Brown.

John Brown, otherwise Jocky Brown, was indicted for assaulting and putting in Fear John Walter, near Bursted, and robbing him of twelve Guineas in Gold, and twelve Pounds in Silver, on the 12th of October, 1748.

John Walter deposed, that riding along the Road near Burstead, about Seven o'Clock, at Night, the 12th of October, he was stopped by four Men; two of them laid hold of the Horse's Bridle, and demanded his Money, which he not delivering, the other two pulled him off his Horse, one of them drew out a Pistol,

[209]

Pistol, and the other aim'd to strike at his Head with a Hanger, which he guarded with his Stick; in the mean while one of the other two took a Canvas Bag with the Money in it out of his Pocket, and afterwards cut his Horse's Bridle, and then they all rode off.

Thomas Dixon*, otherwise Shoemaker Tom, depos'd that himself, the Prisoner, and two others, attack'd the Prosecutor in the Road to Burstead, on the 12th of October, pull'd him off his Horse, and took from him a Canvas Bag, with upwards of twenty Pounds in it of Gold and Silver. They afterwards rode about fourteen Miles farther to a Publick House, where they shifted, meaning, shar'd, the Money among them all four.

Thomas Wickens depos'd, that the Night the Prosecutor, Mr. Walter, was robd'd, the last Witness Dixon, the Prisoner at the Bar, and two others, came to his House about 10 o'Clock at Night; that they call'd for a private Room, where they staid drinking till 12 o'Clock at Night; that they had often been at his House, sometimes two, and sometimes three of them together, but at this Time they were all together.

Sarah Wickens, Wife of the last Witness, depos'd, that the Night Mr. Walter was robb'd, the Prisoner at the Bar, Tho. Dixon,

---

* This Shoemaker Tom has been a notorious Smuggler, but no Murder being charg'd against him, he was by the Court admitted an Evidence.

E e   and

and two others, came to their House at 10 o'Clock at Night ; that they called for a Pen and Ink, and a private Room ; that she waited upon them, and saw them telling out Money in four Parcels ; that there was a great deal of Silver, and some Gold, but could not tell what was the Quantity.

The Prisoner in his Defence, said, that the Witness, Dixon, was a drunken, idle, good for nothing Fellow, and deserved no Credit to be given to what he should swear. But as he could call no Witness to disprove the Facts, or justify his Character, and Dixon's Evidence being very circumstantially corroborated by Mr. and Mrs. Wickens, the Jury found him guilty. Death.

Lawrence Kemp, and Thomas Kemp, were indicted for forcibly entering the Dwelling-House of Richard Havendon, of Heathfield, disguised, and armed with Fire-Arms and Cutlasses, putting him in Fear of his Life, and taking from his Person eleven Shillings and Six-pence, and afterwards, with Violence, seizing and carrying away from his Dwelling-House, thirty five Pounds in Money, two Silver Spoons, three Gold Rings, a two-handled Silver Cup, and a Silver Watch in a Tortoiseshell Case, the 2d of November, 1748.

Richard Havendon deposed, that the 2d of November last, about seven at Night, he heard

heard somebody whistle at his Door, and going out to see who was there, four Men with Crapes over their Faces seiz'd him, put a Pistol to his Breast, and said they wanted Money; upon which he gave them eleven Shillings and Six-pence out of his Pocket, but they said that would not do, and took him with them into the House; when they came in, they called for Candles, and one of them holding a Pistol to his Breast, staid with him below Stairs while the rest went up, where they staid a considerable Time, and then came down Stairs with what they had got; they then took him with them to the Place where they had put their Horses, and swore they would carry him away with them, unless he would tell them where the rest of his Money was, for they were sure he had more than what they had got; But when they were got upon their Horses, they bid him good Night, and went away and left him. When he came back to his own House again, he found they had broke open two Doors, two Trunks, and a Box, and taken away the Money and Things mentioned in the Indictment. Being asked what he was doing when they whistled at the Door, said, he was churning.

Francis Doe, an Accomplice in the said Robbery, being sworn, deposed, that he, John Mills, alias Smoaker, (who was convicted for the Murder of Hawkins) and the two Prisoners at the Bar, agreed to go and rob the Prosecutor's House. That on the 2nd of November they all four, with their Faces cover'd with Crape, came to his House, and whistled at the Door; that when the Prosecutor came out, they seiz'd him, and demanded his Money; that the Prosecutor gave them eleven Shillings and Six-pence out of his Pocket; that then they went into the House, and Lawrence Kemp, one of the Prisoners, stood Centry over the Prosecutor, whilst he, this Witness, with Mills and Thomas Kemp, the other Prisoner, went up Stairs, forced open two Doors, two Trunks, and a Box, and took thereout several Pieces of Gold and Silver, to the Amount of five or six and thirty Pounds, together with some Rings, Spoons, and a Watch. That when they came down Stairs, they took the Prosecutor with them to where their Horses stood, and threaten'd they would carry him away with them, unless he would discover where the rest of his Money was, for they were sure he had more in the House. That upon his declaring he had no more, they let him go home, mounted their Horses, and rode away. Upon shifting, that is, sharing the Money, he had eight or nine Pounds for his Share. That Lawrence Kemp, one of the Prisoners at the Bar was to sell the Watch, Rings, &c. and to divide the Money between them but he never did, as he knew.

Jacob

[213]

Jacob Pring deposed, That he went down to Bristol, to meet with, and bring up John Mills otherwise Smoaker. That when he was there, he met with the two Prisoners at the Bar, who agreed to come up with them. That on the Road, talking together of their Exploits, the two Prisoners owned to him their robbing the Farmer at Heathfield. That they said the old Man was churning when they came to his House. That they craped their Faces over, and took out of the House about five or six and thirty Pounds, besides a Watch, Rings, Spoons, and a Silver Cup.

Being asked by the Court, how they came to be so free as to confess a Robbery to him which must affect their Lives? he said, that he, the two Kemps, and Mills, alias Smoaker, had agreed to go robbing on the Highway, and to break open Houses; that the Prisoners bragged of this amongst many other Robberies they had committed.

Being asked by the Court, whether he had repented of the Agreement that he had so made, he said that he had no such Intention, but that it was only a Feint, and that he went down to Bristol on Purpose to bring up Mills, that he might be apprehended. That there meeting with the Kemps also, and hearing of this Robbery at Heathfield, resolved to do all in his Power to allure them to his
House,

House, in order to get them apprehended as well as Mills.

The Prisoners being call'd upon to make their Defence, both said, they knew nothing of the Robbery, and the Prisoner, Tho Kemp, said, that they never made any such Confession to the Evidence Pring, but that Pring own'd to them, that he, together with John Mills, alias Smoaker, Francis Doe, and Jocky Brown, were all the Persons who robb'd the Farmer at Heathfield.

Being ask'd whether they had any Witness to prove what they had asserted, or where they were when the Robbery was commited? They said they had no Witnesses, for that they had no steady, meaning, no certain, Place of Abode, for two Years past: Upon which the Jury found them both Guilty. Death.

Robert Fuller, was indicted for assaulting William Wittenden, in an open Field, near the King's Highway, putting him in Fear of his Life, and taking from the said William Wittenden, Seven Shillings and Seven-pence Halfpenny, the 13th of last November.

William Wittenden depos'd, That coming a-cross a Field, near Worth, the Prisoner at the Bar, who was on Horse-back, stopp'd him, and enquir'd the Way to Worth; that this Witness directed him; then the Prisoner asked ask'd if he had any Money? he answer'd, No. The Prisoner replied, Damn you, you have, and I will have it, and then pull'd out a Pistol, and put it to his Breast; that then this Witness pull'd out a little Bag, in which was 7s. 6d. in Silver, and three Half-pence, which the Prisoner snatched from him, and then rode away.

Being asked by the Court, if he was sure the Prisoner was the Man that robbed him? answered, yes, he was very sure, and that he saw him ride by him the next Day, in Company with another Man.

The Prisoner in his Defence said, That the Prosecutor declared when he came to see him in the Prison, that he did not know him; and to prove this, called William Cooper, who being sworn, deposed, that the Day before, the Prisoner at the Bar, with two other Prisoners, were put into a Room; that the Prosecutor came in and said, he knew no-body there.

The Prosecutor being ask'd, how many Prisoners he saw in that Room? said, he saw but two, and that afterwards he went into another Room where all the Prisoners were, and did not see any Body there he knew, but turning on his Right Hand he saw the Prisoner standing behind him, and he said, This is the Man that robbed me.

Mr.

[216]

Mr. Rackster deposed, that he was in the Room the first Time the Prosecutor saw the Prisoners, that there were indeed three Prisoners in the Room, but that the Prosecutor saw but two, which stood before him; for that the Prisoner at the Bar stood behind him, which was the Reason that he did not see him then.

The Prisoner being asked, if he had any Witnesses to his Innocence or Character, answered that he had none; upon which the Jury found him guilty. Death.

Richard Savage was indicted for stealing out of the Lewis Waggon 22 Yards three Quarters of Scarlet Cloth, 26 Yards of blue Cloth, the Property of Thomas Friend of Lewis, and a Box, in which were contained 2 Silk Gowns, and two Guineas, the Property of a Person unknown, April the 5th, 1748.

Mr. Friend deposed, that he knew his Servant put up the Cloth, and that he ordered it to be carried to the Waggon.

William Brown, Servant to Mr. Friend, deposed, that he delivered the Cloth to the Carrier's Man.

Matthew Comber, the Carrier's Man, said he received the Cloth from the last Witness, That on the 5th of April last, he was set to watch the Waggon all Night at Chailey; that
two

two Men came up to him about Ten o'Clock at Night, enquiring what Waggon it was; on his telling them, they took him away about 200 Yards from the Waggon, where one of them kept him Prisoner with a Pistol at his Breast; that then came up seven more Men, who got off their Horses, and left them at some Distance from the Waggon, with one Man to take care of 'em. That the rest of the Men went up to the Waggon, and cut the Cords, threw off some Wool-packs, and then threw some Boxes, and other goods out of the Waggon; that they broke open the Boxes, took out the Goods, loaded their Horses and went their Way.

Thomas Winter, otherwise Coachman, an Accomplice, deposed, that on the 5th of April last, he and Shoemaker Tom, with the Prisoner at the Bar, and several others, met at Deval's House at Bird's Hole, and agreed to go out and rob a Waggon that was loaded with wreck'd Goods; that about Ten o'Clock at Night the came all together upon Chailey Common, where they took the Carrier's Man Prisoner, and one of them kept him so, while the rest went and rifled the Waggon. That they broke open several Boxes and Parcels, and took away a large Parcel of Scarlet Cloth, and another large

Parcel of Blue Cloth, and a Box with two Silk Gowns and two Guineas in it, with other Goods. That after they had loaded their Horses, they rode away to Bird's Hole, near Devil's Ditch, where they shared the Goods; that the Prisoner at the Bar was with them in the Robbery, and had a Share of the Goods.

Thomas Dixon, otherwise Shoemaker-Tom, another Accomplice, deposed, That he and Winter, and several others, met together at Deval's House at Bird's-Hole, and agreed to go and rob the Waggon, as mentioned by the last Evidence; that there they laid hold of the Carrier's Man, took him some Distance from the Waggon, and set one of their Number as a Guard over him; that they then plundered the Waggon and took the Cloth and other Things mentioned in the Indictment; that having loaded their Horses, they made the best of their Way to Bird's-Hole, and in a Ditch, near that Place, they divided the Spoil.

Being asked by the Court, if the Prisoner at the Bar was with them at the Time of their committing the Robbery, said, he believed he was, but was not sure; but that he was very sure that he was present at the Time of sharing the Goods, and that he had his Share in the Dividend; and that this Witness sold

sold his Share to the last Evidence Thomas Winter.

The Prisoner in his Defence denied being any Ways concerned in the Robbery; but had no Witnesses to call to contradict the Facts as sworn by the Witnesses for the Prosecution. The Jury brought him in Guilty of the Indictment, which was only laid for single Felony. Transportation.

Mr. Friend, the Prosecutor of Savage, laid the Indictment for a single Felony, because he did not care to take Life away; but the Trial had not been over an Hour, before he was informed by Winter and Shoemaker Tom, that Savage had been concern'd with them in many Things; and that when Savage liv'd as a Servant to Mr. Friend's Brother, to look after and manage a Farm for him, that was fallen upon his Hands, by a Tenant leaving it, that Savage used to entertain them all, which was a Gang of about twelve or thirteen, where they used to come with their Goods, and he found the Horses in Hay and Corn, and them with Victuals and Drink; and they gave him Tea and Brandy for it, which he sold for his own Use. He receiv'd Sentence of Transportation, but is ordered to be stopped, in order to be tryed next Assizes for another Fact.

[220]

Having now given an Account of the Trials of all the seven Smugglers at East-Grinsted, six of whom were executed for the several Crimes they stood convicted, we shall now proceed to give an Account of their Behavionr and last dying Words.

John Brown, alias Jockey Brown, about 33 Years of Age, was born of honest Parents in the County of Sussex, who gave him a tolerable Education; but he had followed Smuggling for many Years, and being apprehensive of being taken up for that Crime, he absconded from his Home, and lurked about; and being acquainted with Winter, commonly called the Coachman, Shoemaker Tom, who was Evidence against him at his Trial, Fuller, and the two Kemps, his Fellow Sufferers, and many more Smugglers, many of whom were out-law'd, they all agreed to rob on the Highway and break open Houses in order to support themselves, being afraid to go a Smuggling; but they did that sometimes when they could get any body that they could trust to take the Goods. He refused to make a general Confession, but did not deny being concerned in robbing Mr. Walter on the Highway near Bursted, for which he suffered.

He exclaimed against Mr. Wickins and his Wife, who gave Evidence against him at his
Trial,

[221]

Trial, and said he had never done them any Harm.

He was taken up at first on Suspicion of being a Smuggler with Richard Mills, who was executed at Chichester, Richard Perrin, alias Payne, Thomas Kingsmill, alias the Staymaker, and William Fairall, alias the Shepherd, the three last now under Condemnation in Newgate for breaking open his Majesty's Warehouse at Poole ; and being carried before Justice Hammond in the Borough of Southwark, he commited them all five to the County Goal for Surry, from whence he was remov'd by a Habeas Corpus to East Grinstead to take his Trial.

He was not so very penitent as a Person should be under his unhappy Circumstances, but he frequently pray'd to God to forgive him; and lamented most for the Disgrace he had brought upon his Family.

Lawrence Kemp, & Thomas Kemp, two Brothers, whose Trials have been before related, refus'd to give any Account of themselves, only that they were born near Hawkhurst in Kent, and that they had been Smugglers for many Years, and had committed many Robberies, but said they never were concern'd in any Murder.

Thomas Kemp being ask'd if he was guilty of the Indictment he was try'd upon at the
Old

Old Bailey before he broke out of Newgate, he at first did not Care to answer the Question, but at last said he was.

They both married two Daughters of a Farmer about two Years since, near Nettlebed, in Oxfordshire; but as the Father of the unhappy two young Women lives in good Reputation, and the Women themselves having the Character of very virtuous Persons, we think it not proper to mention any Particulars concerning them, their own Misfortunes being sufficient to trouble them.

As to Thomas Kemp, he broke out of Newgate soon after he was tryed and acquitted at the Old Bailey, being charged with a large Debt due to the Crown; the Circumstances attending his Escape being somewhat more than common, we shall here insert them.

Thomas Potter and three other Smugglers came into the Press-Yard of Newgate to see Thomas Kemp, and William Grey, who was also one of the Hawkhurst Gang, when they agreed at all Hazards to assist in getting them out; and accordingly the Time was fixed, (Kemp having no Irons, and Grey had his so managed as to let them fall off when he pleased) and Potter and the other three came to the Press-Yard Door, and rung the Bell for the Turnkey to come & let them in; when he came and had unlocked the Door, Potter immediately knocked him down with a
Horse

Horse Pistol, and cut him terribly, when Kemp and Grey made their Escapes, and Potter and his Companions got clear off without being discovered.

There were three other Prisoners got out with them, but were taken directly in the Neighbourhood, having Irons on.

They were both very obstinate Men, and could not be brought to think that Smuggling was a Crime; and when asked if they did not think robbing Farmer Havendon, for which they were convicted was a Crime, they said, yes they did, and begged Pardon of him for it, but that if they had not been obliged to hide themselves from their Home, for fear of being apprehended as Smugglers, they should never have committed Robberies.

Thomas Fuller, about 30 Years of Age, born in Kent, at first denyed the Robbery for which he was to suffer, and often said it was very hard to take away the Life of a Man on the single Testimony of one Person, who was to receive a Reward for so doing; but the Day before his Execution he was brought to a Confession of the Fact, and acknowledged he did commit it in the Manner it was sworn at his Trial.

His Wife attended him at his Trial, and during his Condemnation, for whose Misfortunes he often declared himself sorry, and
said

said he did not value Death, but that he left her to the Reproaches of a censorious World; but begg'd for God sake, that no body would reflect on her or any of her Family, for none of them were ever privy to his wicked Actions.

He acknowledged he had been a Smuggler many Years, and was as deeply concerned as most of them; but that he was not concerned in breaking open the King's Ware-house at Poole, nor in the Murders of Galley and Chater; but confessed he had been a very wicked Sinner.

On Saturday the 1st Day of April last, they were all four taken out of Horsham Goal, (together with Hugh MacCullum a Foot Soldier, who was condemned for a Murder at the said Assizes) and carried to the Gallows, under a strong Guard of Soldiers, where they all seemed much more composed and devout than they had been before. They none of them made any Confessions, only desired all the Spectators to take Warning by their untimely End, particularly all young People.

After they had said their Prayers for some time, they were all tied up to the Gallows, and turned out of a Cart, crying to the Lord to receive their Souls.

We shall now give our Readers, as we promised, an Account of those four notorious Smugglers,

[225]

Smugglers, tried also at the last Assizes at Rochester, for the County of Kent, for diverse Robberies, and were executed on Pickenden Heath, near Maidstone; whose Method of robbing was going in the Evening disguised, and getting into Houses, then binding all the Family, and robbing the same.

Stephen Diprose, and James Bartlett, were indicted, together with John Crumpton, not yet taken, for forcibly entering the Dwelling House of John Rich, of Linton, in the County of Kent, on the 31st of October last, putting him in Fear of his Life, and feloniously taking away 170l. in Money, one small Box, and three Gold Rings.

The Prosecutor deposed, that about Six o'Clock in the Evening, on the 31st of last October, some-body knock'd at the Door; and on his Servant's going to see who it was, four Men rush'd in, all disguised, with Pistols and Cutlasses in their Hands; when they came in they demanded Money, and ask'd him where his Money was, upon which, he, this Deponent, desired they would be easy, and he would give them what he had, but they put one over him, and two of them went and rifled the House; and when they were gone he missed the Money and other Things mentioned in the Indictment.

[226]

Thomas Rogers, who was an Accomplice in the Fact, was next called, who deposed, that he, the Prisoners Stephen Diprose and James Bartlett, and John Crumpton, who is not yet taken, met and agreed to go and get some Money upon the 31st of October last, and accordingly they came to a Resolution, after having proposed many other Things, to go and rob Mr. Rich of Linton, and accordingly they all set out, and when they came at Mr. Rich's Door Diprose knock'd, and the Door was soon open, on which they all rushed in, with Fire Arms and Cutlasses in their Hands, and seized Mr. Rich and all his Family, most of whom they bound, but who they were in particular he could not tell; but he deposed that those that were not bound had one to stand Guard over them; and two of the Gang, which was Crumpton and James Bartlett, rifled the House, and that he believed they took away all the Things mentioned in the Indictment.

Being asked what he meant by saying he believ'd they took away all the Things mentioned in the Indictment, said, that they did not give him nor Diprose a Share of any Thing more than two Gold Rings, and about 70 l. in Money; but that since that Time he had heard by Crumpton, that they took more Money and Goods at Mr. Rich's of Linton, which he and Bartlett had concealed.

Being

Being ask'd if he was sure the Prisoners at the Bar were with him at the Commencement of the Fact, he said, that they all agreed to go to Linton on purpose to rob Mr. Rich, imagining he had got a great deal of Cash by him in his House.

Several of Mr. Rich's Servants were then produced, who deposed to the like Effect of the Theives coming to their Master's House, and acting in the Manner as was before related by the Evidence Rogers; and some of them deposed further, that the Prisoners and Rogers were, they believed, three of the four Men, by their Sizes and Voices, that robbed Mr. Rich's House, and bound most of the Family. Here the Proof for the Prosecutor was ended.

The Prisoners being call'd upon to make their Defence, had little or nothing to say, only deny'd the Fact, and said that Thomas Rogers was a very wicked Fellow, and that they knew nothing of him; and supposed he swore this to get himself at Liberty, and for the sake of the Reward, that was to be paid on their Conviction; but having no Witnesses to prove the contrary of what Rogers had swore, or that they were in any other Place at the Time the Robbery was said to be committed, no body appearing to give them the Character of honest Men; and it likewise appearing by the Testimony of some creditable Witnesses, that they

they and Rogers, and Crumpton, who stands indicted for the same, tho' not yet taken, were all Acquaintance, and frequently together, and reputed all Smugglers, the Jury, without going out of Court, brought them both in Guilty. Death.

William Priggs, and James Bartlett, (the same Bartlett, convicted on the last Indictment) were indicted for forcibly entering the Dwelling-house of John Wright of Snave in the County of Kent, and taking from thence two Bags of Money containing 31l. 7s. 6d.

This Fact was proved upon the Prisoners by the Prosecutor and his Servants, and Rogers an Accomplice; the Prosecutor deposing that he knew the Prisoners again, and were sure they were the Men that robbed him of the two Bags of Money, which contained the Sum mentioned in the Indictment; he further deposed, that when they came into his House they had all three Pistols and Cutlasses in their Hands, and swore they came for Money, and d——n them Money they would have; that they bound him and his Family, and one stood Centry with a Pistol cock'd in his Hand, while the other two went up Stairs and took the Money; that it was Priggs that stood Centry while Bartlett and Rogers went up and took the Money.

The Prosecutor further deposed, that when they had got the two Bags which contained
31 l.

31l. 7s. 6d. they swore they would blow his Brains out if he did not tell them where the rest of his Money was, for they were sure that was not all; that they would destroy the Family if they did not confess where there was more Money, but upon his declaring he had no more in the House, and they making him swear it, they went away; and on going said, if they stirr'd for two Hours, or attempted to call out, they would murder them, and to that End should Stay just by to Watch.

Thomas Rogers, the same Witness as was against Bartlett and Diprose on the last Indictment, deposed, that he and the two Prisoners went and committed the Robbery at Mr. Wright's House at Snave, and bound Mr. Wright and his Family, and took the two Bags of Money mention'd in the Indictment; that they had Crapes with them to put over their Faces, but did not put them on at the committing this Robbery.

Several other Witnesses were produced, who confirmed what had been sworn by the Prosecutor, and Rogers the Accomplice; and the Prisoners having nothing to say or prove in Contradiction to the Evidence that had been given for the Crown, only, in general, said they were innocent of the Crime laid to their Charge, the Jury brought them both in Guilty. Death.

Thomas

Thomas Potter was tried for stealing a Horse; but as he so solemnly declared, and took the Sacrament just before his Execution, that he knew nothing of the Robbery, we shall omit giving Evidence, or mentioning the Names of those concern'd in the Prosecution. The Fact was sworn positively upon him, and he, not being able to prove the contrary, was found Guilty of the Indictment.   Death.

While these Men were under Sentence of Death they were visited frequently by a Reverend Divine of the Town of Maidstone, who endeavour'd to bring them to a true and thorough Repentance of all their past wicked Lives and Actions, being well assured that they had been Smugglers many Years, and that they belong'd to a Gang, who committed many Robberies, such as robbing Houses in the same manner as the Indictments had charged Diprose, Bartlett, and Priggs; and also with having commited many Robberies on the Highway, besides other vile Outrages, as well as Smuggling.

They all behav'd indifferently well under their unhappy Circumstances, much better than those who had been Smugglers generally did, and frequently prayed to God with great Fervency, and were seemingly very sorry for their past mispent lives.

Thomas

Thomas Potter, born at Hawkurst in the County of Kent, about twenty eight Years of Age, declared he had been a very wicked Sinner, and that he had been guilty of all manner of Crimes and Villanies except Murder, which he declared he never was; though he confessed he did design to murder the Turnkey of Newgate, at the Time he went to get Grey and Kemp out of that Goal; but that he was glad it happened no worse to the Turnkey than it did, and that he often prayed the Man might recover of the Wounds he gave him; and that when he heard he was well and abroad again, he said it gave him a great deal of Satisfaction.

He absolutely deny'd the Fact for which he suffered, but acknowledged, that he had committed crimes sufficient to have hanged him by the Law for many Years last past.

He refused to make any particular Confession; but acknowledged that he had been a Smuggler belonging to the Hawkhurst Gang many Years; and that he was well acquainted with the Kemps, Brown and Fuller, that were executed at Horsham ; also with the Mills's who had been executed for the Murder of Chater and Galley; as likewise with Winter the Coachman, and Shoemaker Tom, who were both admitted Evidences against their Companions

panions at Horsham, as has been before related.

William Priggs was born at Selinge, in the County of Kent, of very honest Parents, who gave him very good Education in a common Way, was about thirty Years of Age, and had been a Smuggler some Years last past.

He acknowledged committing the Fact for which he died, as it was sworn against him on his Trial, and begg'd Pardon of the Prosecutor for the great Injury he had done him; as also of others he had in any Ways injured in his Life.

He solemnly declared that it was the evil Gang he kept Company with that persuaded him to commit the Fact he died for, and said he never had been guilty of many Robberies, though he had been a Smuggler many Years.

The Day before his Execution he declared himself truly penitent for all his wicked Crimes he had been guilty of, and said he freely forgave his Prosecutor, as he hoped for Forgiveness from God.

He was asked if he knew of the Robbery of the Revd. Mr. Wentworh, of Brenset, in the County of Kent on the 19th Day of last December, when he declared he did not ; but that he had heard that one Butler was concerned; and for any thing more concerning that Affair he did not know.

James

[233]

James Bartlett, aged forty two Years, was born of very honest Parents at Aknidge, in the County of Kent, who gave him as much Education as their Circumstances would allow them.

He acknowledged the Fact for which he died, but said as Priggs did, that it was evil Company that he had associated himself with, that drew him in to commit those wicked Crimes.

He seemed very obstinate most of the Time of his being under Condemnation, and would not acknowledge himself guilty of any other Robberies ; but said he had been a Smuggler many Years, and did not see any great Crime in that.

He was particularly pressed to know if he was not concerned in any Murders, particularly that of Mr. Castle the Excise Officer, who was shot on Silhurst Common by a Gang of Smugglers, when he, with several other Officers, had seized some Run Goods, to which he would not give a positive Answer, so that there was some Grounds to think he was concerned.

He often said he had not the Sin of Murder to answer for ; but one of his unhappy Companions, and a Fellow Sufferer, said he evaded the Thing, by meaning that no Person was ever murdered by his Hands, but that Bartlett had been concerned where Murder had been committed.

H h   Stephen

Stephen Diprose, born of honest Parents at High Halden, in the County of Kent, 39 Years of Age, acknowledged himself guilty of the Crime for which he was to suffer, and said he had been a wicked Liver, and a most notorious Smuggler, having followed that Employment for a great Number of Years; and that he never entertained a Thought of Smuggling being a Crime till now, and that he was sincerely sorry for all his past Iniquities.

He, as well as Priggs and Bartlett, laid the Blame upon evil Company, and said it was by the Persuasion of some of his Companions that he ever went a robbing; but just before he went out of the Goal to Execution, he confessed it was pure Necessity that obliged him to it, as it was the Case of the rest of his Companions, who were afraid of being apprehended for Smuggling; which if it so happened, they were all dead Men.

He said, that he verily believed, that the Reason why so many notorious Villainies and Murders had been committed by the Smugglers, was owing to their not being safe in appearing publickly.

On Thursday the 3oth of March they were convey'd from Maidstone Goal to Pickenden Heath, the usual Place of Execution.

There

[235]

There were three more Criminals executed with them, that were likewise convicted at the same Assizes at Rochester, viz. Sam. Eling, who was born at Stanmore in Middlesex, about 35 Years of Age, and John Davis, born near Hertford Town, aged 22, as Companions, for a Robbery on the Highway on Bexley Heath; and Richard Watson, born in Yorkshire, who would not tell his Age, but supposed between 30 and 40, also for a Robbery on the Highway. These three Criminals behaved themselves penitent at the Gallows, as indeed they had done during the Time of their lying under Condemnation; and Eling and Davis declared to the last Moment they were both innocent, and that they had never been guilty of any Felonies or Robberies; and forgave their Prosecutor as they expected Forgiveness; and declar'd they died Protestants; as for Watson, he acknowledged his Guilt; and said little more than that he forgave all his Enemies, and died in Charity with all Men.

At the Place of Execution they all behaved penitent, and all declared they died Members of the Church of England. Potter declared to the last Moment he did not commit the Robbery for which he died; and said he freely forgave his Prosecutors, as he hoped for Forgiveness for all his manifold Sins, thro' his Redeemer Jesus Christ. Diprose said just before he was turn'd off, that his greatest

Consolation was, he never committed Murder, or had been concerned at any Time when Murder had been committed. They none added any Thing more to their former Confessions, and having done praying, and singing Psalms, were turned off, crying to the Lord Jesus to receive their Souls.

Having now finished the Accounts of those Smugglers, except those of Kingsmill, alias Staymaker, Fairall, alias Shepherd, Perrin, Glover, and Lillewhite, who were try'd at the Old Bailey for breaking open the King's Custom House at Pool, we shall next proceed to give their Trials, and conclude this Work with a particular Account of their Lives, and last dying Words of Kingsmill, Fairall, and Perrin, who were executed at Tyburn, the first two named now hanging in Chains in Kent.

As to the Life of Kinsgmill it will appear to be very remarkable ; but for that of Fairall the like was never heard before, he being, even, as he acknowledged himself, the wickedest Smuggler living.

Thomas Kingsmill, alis Staymaker, William Fairall, alias Shepherd, Richard Perrin, alias Pain, alias Carpenter, Thomas Lillewhite, and Richard Glover, were indicted and tryed at the Sessions House in the Old Bailey on Friday the 4th of April, 1749, for being concerned, with others, to the Number of 30 Persons, in breaking

[237]

breaking into the King's Custom-house at Poole, and stealing out of thence thirty seven hundred weight of Tea, value 500l. and upwards, Oct. 7, 1747.

The Prisoners being severally arraigned, and all pleading not guilty, the Council for the King opened to the Court and Jury the Nature of the Indictment; then Mr. Banks and Mr. Smythe, two of his Majesty's Council learned in the Law, spoke very particular to the whole Affair, shewing the Enormity of the Crime, as being the most unheard of Act of Villainy and Impudence ever known; and proceeded to call the Witnesses in Support of the Charge.

Captain William Johnson called and sworn. I have a Deputation from the Customs to seize prohibited Goods. On the 22d of September, 1747, I was stationed out of Statnham Bay, just by Poole. I was under the North Shore, and examined a Cutter I suspected to be a Smuggler; after quitting her, I had Sight of the Three Brothers; I discovered her to the Eastward, and after discovering her she put before the Wind at N. N. W. I gave Chase with all the Sail I could make. I chased her from before Five in the Afternoon till about Eleven at Night. After firing several Shot at her, I brought her to, and took Charge of her. I went myself on board, and found she was loaded with Tea, Brandy, and Rum. The Tea

Tea was in Canvas and Oil-skin Bags, over that the usual Package for Tea intended to be run; there was a Delivery of it, forty one hundred three quarters gross weight, in eighty two Parcels; there were thirty-nine Casks, slung with Ropes, in order to load upon Horses, as smuggled Brandy commonly is; there were seven Persons in the Cutter, I cannot say any of the Prisoners at the Bar were there. I carried these Goods to the Custom-house at Poole, and delivered them into the Charge of the Collector of the Customs there, William Milner, Esq; the Tea was deposited in the upper Part of the Warehouse, the Brandy and Rum were lodged in another Part beneath.

William Milner, Esq; was next called and sworn. I am Collector of the Customs at Poole. On the 22nd or 23rd September, Captain Johnson brought a Vessel, whose Name was given to me to be the Three Brothers. She had burden two Ton of Tea, thirty-nine Casks of Brandy and Rum, and a small Bag of Coffee. The Tea was put in the upper Part over the Custom-house all together, except one small Bag, which was damaged, which we put by the Chimney. We made it secure; but it was taken away.

Q. Give us an Account how it was taken away?

Milner. On the 7th of October, between Two and Tthree in the Morning, I had Advice
brought

brought me, by one of the Officers, that the Custom-house was broke open; the Staples were forced out of the Posts; about five or six Feet farther there was another Door broken; at the Door of my Office the upper Pannel was broke in Pieces, as if done with a Hatchet; by which Means they could more easily come at the Lock, which was broke, and another Door, leading up into the Warehouse, was also broken in Pieces. So that there was a free Passage made up to the Tea Ware-house, and the Tea all carried off, except what was scattered over the Door, and one Bag of about five or six Pounds, and the Bag of Coffee. They never attempted the Brandy and Rum. The Reason why some of the Tea was scattered, was most of the Bags had been opened an Inch or two to see what Condition it was in.

Q. Did any body ever come to claim the Brandy and Rum?

Milner. No, for it was condemned in the Exchequer.

Q. Was the Tea in such Sort of Package as the East-India Company have?

Milner. No, Sir, it was packed as is usual for run Tea, and the Brandy was in small Casks all slung ready to fling over the Horses.

The Council for the Crown having done examining Mr. Milner, they proceeded to call several

several Witnesses, who were concerned in the Fact; and in order that nothing but Justice might be done, and the Truth only might appear against the Prisoners, the Witnesses were called in separately, so that Steele, who was the second of them, was not admitted into Court till Raise, who was the first examined, had gone through his Evidence; and Fogden, who was the third and last examined, was likewise not suffered to go into Court till Steele had done.

John Raise was called and sworn; who being ask'd, if he knew the Custom-House at Poole, answered, I do know the Custom-house at Poole.

Q. Do you know any thing of its being broke open?

Raise. It was broke open soon after Michaelmas. I do not know the Day of the Month. It was a Year ago last October. There was Tea taken out of it.

Court. Look at the Prisoners. Do you know either of them?

I know them all.

Q. Give us an Account of what you know about it.

Raise. I was not at the first Meeting. The first Time I was with them about it was in Charlton Forest, belonging to the Duke of Richmond: There was only Richard Perrin of the Prisoners there then. We set our Hands to

[241]

to a Piece of Paper to go and break open Poole Custom-house, and take out the Goods. It was Edmund Richards that set our Names down; some of them met there a Sunday, but I was not then with them; when we met of the Monday at Rowland's Castle, the Prisoners were all there, except Kingsmill and Fairall, and were all armed, when they met, with Blunderbusses, Carbines, and Pistols; some lived thereabouts, and some towards Chichester; so we met there to set out all together. When we came to the Forest of Bare, joining to Horn-Dean, the Hawkhurst Gang met us, the Prisoners Kingsmill & Fairall being with them, and they were 7 in Number, and brought with them, besides the Horses they rode on, a little Horse, which carried their Arms; we went in Company after we were joined, till we came to Lindhurst; there we lay all Day on Tuesday, then all the Prisoners were there: Then we set out for Poole in the Glimpse of the Evening, and we came to Poole about Eleven at Night.

Q. Were all the Prisoners arm'd?

Raise. To the best of my Knowledge all the Prisoners were arm'd both at Horn-Dean in the Forest of Bare, and at Lindhurst; and when we came near the Town of Poole, we sent two Men to see if all things were clear for us to go to work, in breaking the Ware-house, &c. The Men were Thomas Willis, & Thomas

mas Stringer; Thomas Willis came to us, and said, there was a large Sloop lay up against the Key; she'll plant her Guns to the Custom-house Door, and tear us in Pieces, so it cannot be done. We were turning our Horses to go back, when Kingsmill and Fairall, and the rest of their Countrymen said, if you will not do it, we will go and do it ourselves, as being stout resolute Men, and never daunted. This was the Hawkhurst Gang. John and Richard Mills were with them: We call them the East-country People; they were fetched to help to break the Custom-House. Some Time after this, while we were consulting what we should do, Thomas Stringer returned and said the Tide was low, and that the Vessel could not bring her Guns to bear to fire upon us. Then we all went forward to Poole. We rid down a little back Lane on the left Side the Town, and came to the Sea-side. Just by this Place we quitted our Horses, Richard Perrin & Thomas Lillewhite staid there to look after them.

Court. Why did you leave Perrin and Lillewhite with the Horses, more than any body else?

Raise. Because Perrin was troubled some times with the Rheumatism, and not able to carry the Goods so well as the rest, and Lillewhite was a young Man, and had never been with us before.

Court

A Representation of yᵉ Smuggler's breaking open yᵉ KING'S Custom-House, at POOLE.

Court. Well, go forward with your Evidence.

Raise. We went forward, and going along, we met a Lad, a Fisherman, going to fish, we kept him Prisoner. When we came to the Custom-house, we broke open the Door of the Inside; and when we found where the Tea was, we took it away. There was about thirty-seven hundred three quarters. We brought it to the Horses, and slung it with the Slings, and loaded our Horses with it; the Horses were, as near as I can guess, two or three hundred Yards off the Custom-House. We sacked it in what we call Horse-sacks to load.

Court. Were all the Prisoners at the Bar, or which of them, present at the loading the Horses?

Raise. All the five Prisoners were there, I am sure; and after we loaded all the Horses we went to a Place call'd Fordingbridge, there we breakfasted, and fed our Horses. There were thirty-one Horses, and thirty men of us; the odd Horse was that for the East-Countrymen to carry their Arms.

The Council for the King having done with this Witness, those of the Council for the Prisoners got up; and as Mr. Crowle was for Perrin, Mr. Carew for Glover, and Mr. Spilltimber for Lillewhite, the Court advised them to ask such Questions only as related to the Prisoner they were retained for.

Cross-examin'd by Lillewhite's Council.

Q. Did you see either of the Prisoners assist in breaking the Custom-house?

Raise. I saw Fairall and Kingsmill carry Tea from the Custom-house to the Horses. When we came back to a Place called Brook, there we got a Pair of Steelyards, and weighed the Tea, and equally divided to each Man his Share; it made five Bags a Man, about twenty-seven Pound in a Bag; the two Men that held the Horses, which were Lillewhite and Perrin, had the same Quantity.

Q Were you all arm'd, are you sure?

Raise. There were twenty of us all arm'd at Rowland's Castle. Richard Perrin had a Pair of Pistols tied round his Middle.

Q. Had Lillewhite Arms?

Raise. Lillewhite lay at my House on Sunday Night, and another Man with him; their Horses were in my Stable.

Q. Give me an Answer to my Question: Are you sure that Lillewhite had Arms about him when you left him to hold the Horses?

Raise. I cannot tell; I cannot be quite certain.

Q. Was Lillewhite ever with you, before or since that Time?

Raise

Raise. No, never as I know of; I never heard he was a Smuggler.

Cross-examined by Glover's Council.

Q. Was Glover ever reputed a Smuggler before, or did he ever act as such?

Raise. No, not as I know of, neither before or since. Richard Perrin was the Merchant that went over to Guernsey to buy this Cargo of Brandy, Rum, and Tea. I paid him Part of the Money as my Share to go. He told me, after the Goods were taken, and put on boad another Vessel, that he had lost the Tea by the Swift Privateer, Captain Johnson.

Q. Did you never hear that Glover was forced to go against his Consent by Richards his Relation?

Raise. No, I did not hear any such Thing. Edmund Richards brought him, and I never knew him do any thing but this Time.

Cross-examined by Perrin's Council.

Q. Are you sure that Perrin was armed, particularly when he was with the Horses?

Raise. Yes, he was, and was armed all the Way we went from the Forest of Bare, and at that Place too.

Q. You say Perrin was troubled with the Rheuma-

Rheumatism : Why would you take a Man with you, that could not help you to carry the Goods off.

Raise. I dont know ; I am sure he was with us, and had his Share of the Tea when we divided it at Brook.

William Steele was then called, who appearing, was sworn.

William Steele. When I came Home, I was told the Goods were taken by Captain Johnson. The first time we met, I cannot say any of the Prisoners were there. When we met in Charlton Forest at the Center-tree, I believe Richard Perrin was there ; there were a great many of us there ; this was some Time in October ; we met to conclude about getting this Tea out of Poole Custom-house. We came to some Conclusion there ; from thence we came to Rowland's Castle on a Sunday in the Afternoon ; there were about twenty of us ; I think Thomas Lillewhite was there.

Q. Were there any of your Company armed?

Steele. I cannot say there were any Arms there on the Sunday. On the Monday in the Afternoon, some time before Sun-set, when we set out, every Man was armed.

Q. How came they by their Arms?

Steele. They had them from their own Houses, as far as I know. I do not remember one Man without; some had Pistols, some Blunder-

Blunderbusses; all the Hawkhurst Men had long Arms slung round their Shoulders, and Fairall, alias Shepherd, had an Hanger. We went from Rowland's Castle; and when we came to the Forest of Bare, we were joined by the Hawkhurst Gang; this was of a Monday Night. The Prisoners Kingsmill & Fairall were Part of the Hawkhurst Gang that joined us, and had with them a little Horse which brought their Arms, and would follow a grey Horse one of them rode on; there were about seven of them.

We went from Dean to Lindhurst, and, when we set out from thence to Poole, we were all armed; we all looked at our Fire-arms to see if they were primed.

Court. When you looked at your Arms to see if they were primed at Dean, are you sure all the Prisoners were there, or which of them?

Steele. They were all five there at that Time, and we went together till we came near Poole; when Stringer and Willis went forward to see how the Way stood, and to make Observations if any body was about the Custom-house; and when we came within about a Mile of the Town, * Willis and Stringer came and met us, and one of them

* Willis and Stringer stand both Indicted for the Murders of Galley and Chater.

said,

said, it was impossible to be done. We turned our Horses again, and came to a little Lane, and every Man got off, and tied our Horses up to a Rail, which was put along a sort of a Common. There were thirty one Horses, we left them under the Care of Thomas Lillewhite and Perrin; we every Man went to the Custom-house, and broke it open. I, and another, went to the Key, to see that no body came to molest us. When I came back again, the Custom-house was broke open; they said it was done with Iron Bars. They were carrying the Tea when the other Man and I came to them.

Court. Who do you mean were carrying the Tea?

Steele. All that went on purpose to break the Custom-house open, I don't mean any in particular.

Court. Were any of the Prisoners there?

Steele. Yes, Glover, Kingsmill and Fairall; Lillewhite and Perrin being still with the Horses. When we came we found the Strings, and tied it together, and carried it away to a gravelly Place, where we laid it down. There we fetched our Horses to the Place, and loaded them, and carried it away. Then we went to a Place called Fordingbridge, where we baited our Horses, and refreshed ourselves. We loaded, and went for a Place called Sandy-Hill; but at a Place called Brook,
before

before we came to this Place, we got two Pair of Steelyards, and weigh'd the Tea, and it came to five Bags a-piece.

Q. Did you carry the Tea to your Horses, or did you bring the Horses to the Tea?

Steele. we carried the Tea to a plain Place convenient for loading. Then we brought the Horses forward to be loaded.

Here Raise was call'd again, as he had said they carried the Tea to the Horses.

Q. to Raise. Did you carry the Tea to the Horses?

Raise. I had been employed at the Customhouse to tie up the Tea; and, when I came, the Horses were with the Tea.

Cross-examined by Lillewhite's Council.

Q. Did you ever know Lillewhite before?
Steele. I have known him, and been acquainted with him four or five Years.

Q. Who came there first he or you?
Steele. He was there first.

Q. Was Lillewhite ever a Smuggling with you before this Time.

Steele. Not as I know of.

Q. Was he ever reputed a Smuggler before this Affair happened.

Steele. Not as I know of.

Q Do you think when Lillewhite went with you, that he knew what you were going about?

Steele. I think he did ; we talk'd openly of it ; but I cannot swear he did.

Q. Don't you know that Lillewhite was ask'd only to take a Ride with you, and that he did not know what you were going upon, till you came to the Forest of Bare.

Steele. I can't say any such Thing ; he join'd us at Rowland's Castle.

Q. You say the Hawkhurst Gang join'd you on the Forest of Bare, and had a little Horse with them.

Steele. Yes.

Q. What Arms were upon that little Horse?

Steele. I think there were seven long Muskets on him.

Q. Were they Arms for you?

Steele. We had Arms before that ; they were brought for their own Use.

Q. Had Lillewhite any Arms when holding the Horses?

Steele. I cannot say that he had.

Q. Did you all put down your Names on a Piece of Paper to go upon this Affair?

Steele. Each Man's Name was put down by Edmund Richards.

Q. Was Lillewhite's Name put down?

Steele. I cannot say it was.

Cross-examined by Glover's Council.

Q. Was Glover ever concerned in Smuggling before this? Steele.

Steele. No, I believe he never was before or since.

Q. Did you ever hear he went with Reluctancy, and against his Will?

Steele. As to that, I never heard he did; but I believe Richards forced him to it; this I know, Glover lived in Richards's House, and I believe Richards was the Occasion of his going with us *.

Q. Who was your Commander?

Steele, There was no-body took the Lead one more than the other.

The Council for the King then call'd Robert Fogden, who being come into Court, was sworn.

Robert Fogden. I remember the Time the Tea was seized upon. I was at the Consultation in Charlton Forest; there we concluded to go after the Tea; this was at a n oted Tree that stood in the Forest, called the Center-Tree. I do not know whether either of the Prisoners were there. I was not at Rowland's Castle; I was with others of the Company, on a Common just below, for we met at both Places, and then met all together at a Place appointed in the Forest of Bare.

Q. Were any of the Prisoners at the House you was at.

Fogden. No, not one. At the Forest of

* Edmund Richards also stands indicted for being concerned in the Murder of Galley and Chater.

Bare there were, I believe, all the five Prisoners. We met together at a lone Place there; we staid there till the Hawkhurst Men came to us ' then there were thirty of us in Number. The Prisoners Kingsmill and Fairall came with the Hawkhurst Gang, and were Part of that Gang.

Q. Were you all armed?

Fogden. To the best of my Knowledge we were all armed.

Q. For what Purpose did you meet there?

Fogden. We were going to fetch away the Tea that had been taken from us by Captain Johnson, and lodged in the Custom-house at Poole.

Q. How did you take it?

Fogden. By Force; we went from thence to Lyndhurst; we got there in the Night, just as it was light. We staid there till near Night again; then in the Night we went to Poole, and went to the Backside of the Town, and left our Horses in a little Lane. I never was at Poole before this, or since; I believe we left our Horses about a Quarter of a Mile out of Town. We left them to the Care of two Men, Perrin and Lillewhite. Then we went and broke open the Custom-house. I saw the Door broke open with two Iron Bars.

Q. Where did you get them?

Fogden. I cannot tell.

Q. Where did you find the Tea lodged?

Fogden.

Fogden. It was in the Top of the Warehouse.

Q. Were any of the Prisoners at the Bar concerned in it?

Fogden. They were there, and did assist as the rest, except the two that held the Horses. We brought the Horses to a Place near, and then carried the Tea to them. It was a very narrow Lane where we stopped first, and we brought the Horses up to a more open Place for loading.

Q. Did the Prisoners at the Bar help you load?

Fogden. Yes, all of them.

Q. Did you put an equal Quantity on each Horse?

Fogden. We distributed it as near as we could. There was one little Horse that carried the Arms, had not so much as the other Horses had on them. Every Horse there was loaded with Tea; from thence we went to a little Town called Fordingbridge; at the next Place we stopped, we weigh'd the Tea with two Pair of Steelyards; for we thought it was not equal, some was shattered out of some of the Bags. Then we divided it as equal as we could; they were quartern Bags, each Prisoner had five Bags.

Q. When did you see Lillewhite first?

Fogden. In the Forest. I never saw him before.

Q. Was

Q. Was he there before or after you?

Fogden. I cannot tell.

Q. Did you hear any Threats, if any should discover this Affair, what should be done to them?

Fogden. No, Sir.

Q. Had Lillewhite Arms when left with the Horses?

Fogden. I believe he had not.

Q. Was Lillewhite ever with you a Smuggling before?

Fogden. No, never as I know of.

Q. Was Glover ever with you a Smuggling before?

Fogden. No, never as I know of.

The Council for the King resting their Proof here, the Prisoners were severally call'd upon to make their Defences; when Kingsmill and Fairall said, they had nothing to say, only that they knew nothing of the Matter.

Perrin having retained Council for him, called the following Persons to his Character.

John Guy. I have known Perrin almost twenty Years; he is a Carpenter, and always bore a very good Character among his Neighbours; I never heard he neglected his Business.

Q. Did

Q. Did you never hear he was a Smuggler?

Guy. I have known him these fifteen or sixteen Years, he always bore a very good Character. I never heard in my Life of his neglecting his Business, and going a Smuggling.

Q. Did you never hear he was a Smuggler?

Guy. No never, but by Hearsay, as Folks Talk.

For Glover, Richard Glover's Defence. I was forced into it by my Brother-in-law Edmund Richards, who threatened to shoot me, if I would not go along with them.

William Tapling. I have known Richard Glover twenty Years. I never heard, before this unhappy Affair, that he was a Smuggler. I believe he never was before. I know his Brother-in-law Richards ; and that Glover was about two Months with him. Richards is a notorious wirked, swearing Man, and reputed a great Smuggler ; I can't help thinking he was the Occasion of Glover's acting in this.

Henry Housel. I have known Glover of a Child ; he was a sober young Lad ; I never knew him otherwise, or did I ever hear him swear an Oath in my Life.

Q. Did you never hear he was a Smuggler?

Hou-

[256]

Housel. Never before this. He lived with his Father till the Year 1744. His Father dying, he followed his Business till August 1747. He went in the Begining of June to that wicked Brother's House, and was there about two Months. He went after that to live Servant with the Rev. Mr. Blagden; after that he got into Deptford yard, and there he continued ever since, till taken up, articled to a Ship-wright. This Affair was in the very Time he was at his Brother-in-law's House.

John Grasswell. I have known Glover these twelve Years and upwards. I believe he never was guilty of Smuggling before this? his Character is exceeding good. I never knew him frequent bad Company, or guilty of drinking or swearing an Oath.

Woodruff Drinkwater. I have known Glover ever since he was born; I never heard he was reputed a Smuggler either before or since, exclusive of this Time; his Temper is not formed for it at all, far from it; after his Father died he was left joint Executor with his Mother, (left in narrow Circumstances) he often came to me on any little Occasion for five or ten Guineas; he always kept his Word; after his Mother married again, there was some Difference in his Family, he went into the Country, and I was very sorry for him at his going to Richards's House, and I cannot think he was voluntarily in this rash action.

Mr.

Mr. Edmonds. I have known Glover ever since the 9th of April last; he came to me and was entered into his Majesty's Yard at Deptford the Day following; he bore a good Character before, and during the Time he has been with me he has behaved very well and sober; he obtain'd a good Character of all that knew him; I have had as good an Opinion of him as any Man I know; he was with me till the Day he was taken.

Mr. Dearing. I live in the Parish where this young Man was born. I go there for the Summer Season; I have known him about eighteen Years; I being informed of this bad thing, made me come to London on Purpose to say what I knew of him: We in the Country had great Reason to believe that bad Man Richards had corrupted him; he was a well-behaved Lad before this happened: His Uncle came to me, and the young Man came and begg'd of his Uncle, that he would see out for some Business for him, in some way or other, adding, that he could not bear to live with Richards; I had just hired a Servant, or I had took him, just after this bad Affair happen'd, and he was unfortunately drawn into it.

The Rev. Mr Blagdon. I live at Slendon in Sussex, the Prisoner Glover was my Servant; I knew him and his Family before; he behaved exceeding well with me, as any could, and if he were discharged from this, I would readily take him again; he attended on religious Service publick and private constant; I never heard an ill Word or an Oath from his Mouth, or any thing vulgar.

For Thomas Lillewhite.

His Defence. I was down in that Country, and a Person desired me to take a Ride with him; I agreed upon it, not knowing where they were going; I had no fire-arms, nor was any way concerned.

Fra. Wheeler. I have known Lillewhite about six Years; he always bore a very good Character; was a worthy young Fellow, and brought up in the Farming under his Father, who is a Man in very good Circumstances; he minded his Father's Business very diligently: I have known him refuse going out upon Parties of Pleasure, because he has had Business of his Father's to do; he married since this Affair happened to a Woman of Fortune; I never heard him charged with any such Crime as this before.

Sir Cecil Bishop. The Prisoner married my Housekeeper's Daughter; had not he been a Man of good Character, I should not have been consenting to the Match, which I was; she brought him a good Fortune; he is a deserving young

[259]

young Man, and I cannot think he would be guilty of such a Crime knowingly.

The Evidence being all finished, Sir Thomas Abney summed up the Whole in a very impartial Manner; taking Notice, that in the Case of Lillewhite, if they thought the Evidence that had been given against him, was not quite full, as to his going voluntarily with them, and that he was not armed with Fire-arms, they might acquit him.

The Jury went out of Court, and in about a Quarter of an Hour returned into Court, and gave their Verdict, as follows, viz.

Thomas Kingsmill, William Fairall, and Richard Perrin, guilty, Death.

Thomas Lillewhite, acquitted.

Richard Glover, guilty, but recommended to Mercy by the Jury.

Thomas Lillewhite was immediately discharged out of Court as soon as he was acquitted; and the other 4 received Sentence of Death the next Day, together with seven other Criminals who had been tried and convicted of divers Felonies and Robberies.

While under Sentence of Death, they all four, viz. Kingsmill, Fairall, Perrin, and Glover, behaved much better than they had done before; and particularly Glover and Perrin were very composed and resigned, and constantly prayed and sung Psalms most of the

Night Time ; but Kingsmill and Fairall were not so penitent as Glover and Perrin.

As for Kingsmill and Fairall, they were reckoned two of the most audacious wicked Fellows amongst the Smugglers ; and indeed, their Behaviour while under Confinement plainly shewed it.

The Day they were brought to Newgate by Habeas Corpus, from the County Goal for Surry, which was 3 Days before their Trial, Fairall behaved very bold, after declaring he did not value being hanged ; and said, Let's have a Pipe and some Tobacco, & a Bottle of Wine, for as I am not to live long, I am determined to live well the short Time I have to be in this World. He also behaved very insolently at his Trial ; or in short more properly may be said ignorantly, laughing all the Time at the Witnesses while they were giving their Evidence ; and when taken Notice of by the Court, and reprimanded for his bad Behaviour, it had no Effect on him, for he continued his idle impudent Smiles, even when the Jury brought him in guilty.

At the Time when he received Sentence of Death, when Mr. Recorder, who passed the same on him, & the rest of the Criminals, said these Words; and the Lord hve Mercy on your Souls ; he boldly replyed ; If the Lord has not more Mercy on our Souls, than the Jury has

has had on our Bodies, I don't know what will become of them.

On Thursday the 20th of April, 1749, the Report of these four Criminals was made to his Majesty by Richard Adams, Esq; Recorder, when Kingsmill, Fairall, and Perrin were ordered for Execution at Tyburn on Wednesday the 26th of the same Month; and his Majesty was pleased to grant his most gracious Pardon to Glover, several favourable Circumstances appearing in his Favour; and the Court and Jury having, after his Trial, recommended him to his Majesty for Mercy.

After the dead Warrant came down, Kingsmill and Fairall began to consider their unhappy Circumstances more than they had done before, and always attended divine Service at Chapel, and prayed very devoutly; but retained their former Behaviour of Boldness and Intrepidity, shewing no Fear, and frequently saying, they did not think they had been guilty of any Crime in Smuggling, or in breaking open Poole Custom-house, as the Property of the Goods they went for was not Captain Johnson's, or any body's else, but of the Persons who sent their Money over to Guernsey for them.

Perrin, who was ordered only to be hanged, and afterwards buried, & Kingsmill & Fairall being ordered to be hung in Chains, Perrin was saying to them that he lamented their Cases;

when

when Fairall reply'd, smilingly, in the Presence of many People, We shall be hanging up in the sweet Air, when you are rotting in your Grave.

The Evening before their Execution, after they came down from Chapel, their Friends came to take Leave of them; and Fairall smoked his Pipe very heartily, and drank freely; but being ordered to go into his Cell to be lock'd up, said, why in such Hurry, can't you let me stay a little longer, and drink with my Friends, I shall not be able to drink with them To-morrow Night?

I shall next proceed to give the little Account of these Criminals as given by the Ordinary of Newgate; and afterwards conclude this Book with a Relation of some of the most notorious Actions committed by them, and which have been communicated by their Confederates.

Thomas Kingsmill, alias Staymaker, aged 28, was born at Goodhurst in the County of Kent, a young Fellow of enterprizing Spirit, and for some Years past employed by the Chiefs of the Smugglers, the monied Men or Merchants, as they are usually among themselves called, in any dangerous Exploits or wicked Undertakings. As his Character in general among his own Countrymen was, that of a bold resolute Man, undaunted, and fit for the wicked Purposes of Smuggling; and never intimidated

intimidated, in Case of any Suspicion of betraying their Secrets, ready to oppose King's Officers in their Duty, and being concerned in Rescues of any Sort, or Kind, so he wanted not Business, but was made a Companion for the greatest of them all, and was always at that Service, when wanted and called upon.

He would own nothing of himself, and was scarce to be persuaded that he had done any Thing amiss by following the bad Practices of Smuggling.

He acknowledged that he was present at the Breaking open the Custom House, and that he had a Share of the Tea they took away; and said what was sworn by the Witnesses at the Trial was all Truth; but that they must be bad Men to turn Evidence to take away other Peoples Lives.

William Fairall, alias Shepherd, aged 25, was born at Horsendown-Green, in the County of Kent, bred to no Business, yet I could learn, inured to Smuggling from his Infancy, and acquainted with most of the evil Practices which have been used in those Parts for some Years past. In this Behaviour he seemed equally as well qualified for the Work as was Kingsmill, if any Thing, he had the Advantage; and 'tis generally believed that they were concerned together in most, if not all their Undertakings. Fairall at his Trial seemed to shew the utmost Daringness, and Unconcern,

Unconcern, even shewing Tokens of Threats to a Witness, as he was giving his Evidence to the Court, and standing all the while in the Bar with a Smile or rather a Sneer upon his Countenance. He came also to the Gang with Kingsmill to the Forest of Bare, and was one of the forwardest and most busy among the Company. Yet would he not own against himself any one Thing that he had done amiss, for which his Life should be at Stake. However, his own Countrymen were glad when he was removed from among them, because he was known to be a desperate Fellow, and no Man could be safe, who Fairall should once think had done any Thing to offend him.

Richard Perrin, alias Paine, alias Carpenter, aged 36, was born near Chichester, in Sussex; being bred a Carpenter, was looked upon as a good Workman, and had pretty Business, till the Use of his Right Hand being in a great Measure taken away by being subject to the Rheumatism, he thought proper to leave that Trade, and to take to Smuggling. He was esteemed a very honest Man as to every other Affair of Life, and was therefore often entrusted by others to go over the Water to buy Goods for them, and for himself to; he traded in that Way for Brandy and Tea. And he was the Man that went over for this very Cargo of Goods that was rescued

rescued from Poole Custom-House. Having talked to them several Times, each by himself and all together, neither of them all three would own any thing ; but said they knew best what they had done, and for what was amiss they would seek God's Forgiveness, and continued thus to declare to the last. They have indeed appeared very devout, ever since they received Sentence of Death; they were attentive to public and private Prayer.

Having now given the Ordinary of Newgate's short Account of these Criminals, I shall proceed to give some Account of such of their wicked Actions as have come to our Knowledge.

About 2 Years since William Fairall was apprehended as a Smuggler in Sussex, and being carried before James Butler, Esq; near Lewis ; was ordered by that Gentleman to be brought to London under a strong Guard of Soldiers, in order to be try'd for the same. They brought him quite safe to an Inn in the Borough over Night, in order to carry him before Justice Hammond the next Morning, but he found Means to escape from the Guards ; and seeing a Horse stand in Blackman-street, with a Bridle and Saddle on, he got upon it, and rode away, though in the Presence of several People.

He made the best of his Way down into Sussex, to his Gang, who were surprized at seeing him, knowing he was carried to London under a strong Guard of Soldiers but 3 Days before; but he soon informed them how he got away, and of his lucky Chance of stealing the Horse.

They were no sooner met than he declar'd Vengeance against Mr. Butler, and propos'd many Ways to be revenged: First to destroy all the Deer in his Park, and all his fine Trees, which was readily agreed to by them all; but Fairall, Kingsmill & John Mills, lately executed on Slendon Common, and many more of them, declared that would not satisfy them, nothing but Mr. Butler's Destruction should satisfy them; and accordingly they propos'd to set Fire to his Seat, one of the finest in the County of Sussex, and burn him in it; but this most enormous wicked Proposal was objected to by three of the Gang, namely Thomas Winter, alias the Coachman, one Stevens, and one Slaughter, commonly called Captain Slaughter, who protested against setting the House on Fire, or killing the Gentleman; and great Disputes arose among them, and they parted at that Time without putting any of their villainous Proposals in Execution: But Fairall, Kingsmill, and some more of the Gang were determined not to let their Resentment drop, & accordingly they got each a Brace of Pistols, and determined to go and way-lay him near his own Park Wall, and shoot him. Accordingly

cordingly they went into the Neighbourhood, when they heard Mr. Butler was gone to Horsham, and that he was expected home that Night, upon which they laid ready to execute their wicked Design; but Mr. Butler, by some Accident, happening not to come home that Night, they were heard to say to each other, Damn him he won't come home to Night, let's be gone about our Business; and so they went away angry at their Disappointment, swearing they would watch for a Month together, but they would have him.

This Affair coming to Mr. Butler's Knowledge, Care was taken to apprehend them if they came again, and they being acquainted therewith, did not care to go a second Time without a Number, but no one would join except John Mills, and Jackson, who was condemned at Chichester for the Murders of Galley and Chater, as not caring to run into so much Danger; and they not thinking themselves, being only four, strong enough, the whole Design was laid aside.

On their being disappointed in their Revenge against Mr. Butler, they were all much chagrined, and Fairall said, D——n him, an Opportunity may happen some Time, that they might make an Example of Mr. Butler, & all others that shall dare presume to obstruct them.

Thomas Winter, and several others of the Smugglers, whose Lives had been sav'd by turning Evidence, said that Fairall and Kingsmill had been the Occasion of carrying several Officers of the Customs and Excise abroad from their Families, for having been busy in detecting the Smugglers, and seizing their contraband Goods.

Fairall and Kingsmill were both concerned with the Gang in Kent, viz. Diprose, Priggs, and Bartlett, in all the Robberies they committed; but as an Account of those have been given before, we think it needless to make a Repetition.

The Morning of their Execution they behaved very bold, shewing no Signs of Fear of Death, and about nine o'Clock, Fairall and Kingsmill were put in one Cart, and Perrin in a Mourning Coach, and conveyed to Tyburn under a strong Guard of Soldiers, both Horse and Foot.

At the Tree they joined in Prayers very devoutly with the rest of the unhappy Criminals who were executed with them, which being ended, and a Psalm sung, they were turned off crying to the Lord to receive their Souls.

The Body of Perrin was delivered to his Friends to be buried; and those of Fairall and Kingsmill were carried to a Smith's Shop in Fetter-Lane, near Holborn, where they were put into Chains; and afterwards put into two Wooden Cases made on Purpose, and conveyed

veyed by some of the Guards, and the Sheriff's Officers for the County of Middlesex, to New-Cross Turnpike in the County of Kent; where they were received by the Officers to the Sheriff of that County, who conveyed them to the Places were they were ordered to be hung up, viz. Fairall on Horsendown Green, and Kingsmill on Gowdhurst Gore, at both which Places they had lived.

Richard Glover, who had received his Majesty's Pardon, was discharged out of Newgate on Wednesday the 3d of May, 1749.

We can with Pleasure inform our Readers, that that notorious wicked Fellow, (Edmund Richards, so often named in this Work, as being concerned in the Murder of Galley and Chater, and also in forcing Richard Glover to go with him and the rest of the Gang to break open Poole Custom-house) is taken, and in safe Custody in Winchester Goal, so there is no doubt but he will meet with a just Reward for all his cruel and enormous Crimes, at the next Assizes for the County of Sussex, to which County Goal he will be removed by Habeas Corpus.

F 1 N I S,

THE INDEX,

OR

CONTENTS.

                                              Page

Galley & Chater coming to Rowland's Castle   4
Consultation to murder Galley & Chater, and throw them down a Well, near Rowland's Castle   7
Jackson's and Carter's Wives present   8
Cruelties began on Galley and Chater by the Smugglers   9
Galley murdered   12
Chater carried to Old Major Mills's, and chained in the Turf-House or Skilling   15
Galley buried in a Sand Hole   16
Consultation to murder Chater   19
Cruelties executed on Chater, by Tapner and Cobby, in the Skilling   23
Chater murdered at Harris's Well   27
A Discovery made of the Murder of Chater   35
William Steele, one of the Gang, taken, who made a full Discovery of the Murder of Galley, likewise   36
John Raise, alias Race, taken, and turns Evidence   37
John Hammond taken   ibid.
John Cobby taken   ibid.
Benjamin Tapner taken   38

	Page
Richard Mills, Jun. taken	38
William Carter and William Jackson taken	ibid.
Old Major Mills taken	39
Trials at large of John Hammond, John Cobby, Benjamin Tapner, William Carter, William Jackson, Richard Mills, sen. and Richard Mills, jun. at Chichester, for the Murder of Daniel Chater,	49
List of the Grand Jury	50
The several Defences of the seven Prisoners	132
	133, 134
Jackson's and Carter's Trials for the Murder of William Galley	137
Judgment of Death passed upon all the seven bloody Criminals	147
The Reverend Mr. Smithe's Account, on visiting them under Condemnation	153
The Rverend Mr. Simon Hughes's ditto	ibid.
Account of their Lives	154
Their Behaviour at the Place of Execution	169
Henry Sheerman's Trial at East-Grinsted, for the Murder of William Galley	172
Account of his Life, Behaviour under Sentence of Death, and at the Place of Execution, with his last dying Words	180
Trial of John Mills, alias Smoaker, for the Murder of Richard Hawkins, at the Dog and Partridge on Slendon Common	188
Remarkable Story of John Mills's being apprehended	201
Account of his Life, Behaviour under Condemnation, and at the Place of Execution	204
Trial of Jockey Brown	208
——— of Lawrence & Thomas Kemp, two Brothers	210
——— of Robert Fuller	214
——— of Richard Savage	216
Account of Jockey Brown's Life	220
——— of Lawrence and Thomas Kemp	221

	Page
Account of Thomas Fuller	223
——- of Stephen Diprose & James Bartlett, condemned at Rochester Assizes for robbing the House of John Rich, of Linton	225
——- of William Priggs, also condemned at Rochester for robbing the House of Mr Wright, of Snave	228
——- of Thomas Potter, condemned at the said Assizes	230
——- of the wicked Lives of Jockey Brown, Lawrence and Thomas Kemp, & Robert Fuller, with their Behaviour under Sentence, and at the Place of Execution.	231
Trials at large of Thomas Kingsmill, William Fairall, Richard Perrin, Thomas Lillewhite, and Richard Glover, at the Session-House in the Old Bailey, for breaking open the King's Custom-House, at Poole in Dorsetshire	236
The Behaviour of Kingsmill, Fairall, and Perrin, under Sentence of Death	257
An Account of the wicked Lives of Kingsmill and Fairall	263

Directions for placing the Cuts.

	Page
Galley and Chater on one Horse, and the Smugglers whipping them, to front	9
Galley and Chater falling off the Horse at Woodash, to front	10
Burying of Galley, to front	16
Chater cut across the Face by Tapner, in Old Mills's Turf-House, to front	23
Chater hanging in the Well in Lady-Holt-Park, to front	27
Richard Hawkins whipped to Death, to front	194
The Smugglers breaking open Poole Custom House, to front	243

[I]

JOB xxix. 14, 15, 16.

I put on Righteousness and it cloathed me, my Judgment was as a Robe and a Diadem.

I was Eyes unto the Blind, and Feet was I to the Lame.

I was a Father to the Poor, and the Cause, which I knew not, I searched out.

THAT *Job* was a Person of great Eminence both for his Birth and Station, that he had the supreme Rule and Government, or was at least a principal Magistrate of the Place he dwelt in, appears plainly from this Chapter, whence the Text is taken. *When I came in Presence,* says he, *the young Men saw me, and hid themselves, and the Aged arose and stood up ; the Princes refrained talking, and the Nobles held their Peace*;

I sat

[2]

I sat as Chief, and dwelt as a King in the Army, and all Men gave attention to my Words, and kept Silence at my Counsel.

But whatever was the particular State of this illustrious Person, whether he was invested with the supreme Power itself, or acted only by Commission under it, this is certain, that the Integrity of his Conduct is a Pattern worthy the Imitation, and was recorded doubtless that it might be imitated by those, who should in After-ages be honoured with the like Employment, and fill the same high Office with himself. *I put on Righteousness and it cloathed me, my Judgment was as a Robe and a Diadem.* Expressing the great Love he had to Justice, and the Pleasure he took in exercising Judgment; that what a Robe, and a Diadem, was usually to other Men, that the doing Justice and Judgment was to Him ; the great Object of his whole Desire, the Thing he principally placed his Glory and Delight in. For that we are thus to understand the Metaphor in the Text, is plain from a like Expression made use of by the Royal Prophet, who, speaking
of

[3]

of the Wicked, says, that he *cloathed himself with Cursing like a Garment:* which Expression in the Verse immediately succeding he explains by telling us, that his *Delight was in Cursing*. So that what we are here to understand of *Job* is, that his greatest Satisfaction and Delight was to administer Justice righteously; that his Sense of true Honour, was not that which reflected from these external Marks of Dignity and State, but which sprang from those Virtues, of which these were but the outward Signs. *He put on Righteouiness as a Garment, and cloathed himself with Judgment, as with a Robe and a Diadem.*

The Things then, which naturally offer themselves to our Consideration from the Words before us, are these three,

First, The Duties, which this great Example represents to us, and which more immediately belong to Magistrates, and those who are invested with publick Authority.

Secondly, How great a Blessing every good Magistrate must be to the State, and Community, whereunto he belongs. And

Thirdly,

Thirdly, The personal Respect and Reverence, with which he ought to be treated upon that Account.

The first then of those Duties to which we are led by this great Example, is that of doing Justice and Judgment with Zeal and Chearfulness. ——– Now Justice is a Virtue that not only in the common Consideration of it is, as every other Virtue is, honourable in itself, and much to be desired for its own Sake; but it is a Virtue so peculiarly necessary for human Society, that it is scarce conceivable how any Society can subsist without it: For the Want of Justice, if it destroys not the very Foundations of Society, at least it deprives us of all the Advantages of it, and renders such political Establishments as best but useless and undesirable Things. A State of Solitude would give more Comfort and Security, than such a State, where the just Claims of Society are defeated by cruel and unrighteous Men, and Oppressions permitted with Impunity; But where Justice is, there the Diligent and Industrious prosper, and the Innocent dwell safely. And therefore the great

great Creator of Mankind, who made them for a social Life, has stamped upon their Hearts this most necessary of all social Virtues, and made it the indispensable Law of their Natures, that they should *do to others*, as they wou'd have others *do to them*. And was this Law but universally and duly kept, it could not fail to promote the Happiness, by its Tendency to preserve the Order of the World: It bindeth up every Hand from doing Violence, and every Heart from forging Deceit; and guards the common Safety of Mankind with this strict Command, that we *render to all their Due, Custom to whom Custom, Honour to whom Honour, Fear to whom Fear.*

Nor let us be so deceived, as to think that our own private Interest is not equally concerned herein, with that of the Publick: For the Good of particular Persons can in no Society be distinguished from the general Good, but is always, and unavoidably, included in it. So that if we wilfully connive at, if we suffer, or neglect to correct Abuses in the Publick, we do what in us lies to lessen our own Security,

curity, and insensibly promote the Ruin of our private Interest and Prosperity.

So much Reason have we to esteem, and to endeavour to secure the Practice of this best of Virtues, if we respect only the Thing itself, and the Benefits thence resulting to ourselves, either singly considered, or in Society. But it is by the righteous and impartial Exercise hereof, that God also is most effectually glorified by us: For then only we can in any Sense be said to promote the Glory, when we strive to imitate the Excellencies of God; and Justice being one of the principal of those moral Excellencies, which he has propounded to us as a Pattern for our Imitation, we do then in an eminent Manner give him the Honour due unto his Name, when we study to be like him in this Perfection of his Nature: when they particularly, who are his Ministers for this very Thing, that is, for the Execution of Justice, endeavour to resemble him, whose Ministers they are, in being Just even as he is Just.

Another Instance which *Job* here gives us of his own Integrity, and wherein He
has

has set us an Example, that we should follow his Steps, is his Forwardness to give Relief and Assistance to the Injured and Oppressed. *I was Eyes unto the Blind, and Feet was I to the Lame : I was a Father to the Poor, and the Cause, which I knew not, I searched out.* —— Every Man, according to his Place and Power, is both in Justice and Charity obliged to use his best Endeavours, and to lay hold on all Opportunities, by all lawful Means, of helping them to Right that suffer Wrong: of protecting the Innocent from Injuries, and securing them from the Oppressions of *blood-thirsty and deceitful Men.* It is our Duty every one to exert the utmost of his Strength to deliver the Oppressed, and it is extremely criminal to be *weary, or faint in our Minds*, for fear of the Oppressors, or *forbear to deliver those who are ready to be slain.* That we may see more clearly then the Necessity of this Duty, and be animated to a chearful and conscientious Performance of it, there are various Reasons that deserve our Attention: But those which more especially demand it, and which, if

we

we have any Sense of Religion left, will have their Influence upon us, are the Command and Example of God himself.

And First, we have God's positive and express Command for this Purpose. —— It is the general and fundamental Law of our Religion, the Ground and Basis of all moral Virtue, that *thou shalt love thy Neighbour as thyself.* And how can we more effectually fulfil this second great Commandment of the Law, than by employing the Power God has put into our Hands, of whatever kind it be, for our Neighbour's Good; for securing his Person from Violence, and his Property from Fraud and Rapine?

But besides the Command of God, we have his Example also for the Performance of this Duty. This the Holy Psalmist has set clearly before us, to the end that we may be *Followers* of him herein, *as dear Children. Now for the comfortless Trouble's Sake of the Needy, and because of the deep Sighing of the Poor, I will up, saith the Lord, and will help every one from him that swelleth against him, and will set them at Rest.* And if the

the great God of Heaven and Earth, he who *hath his Dwelling so high*, does yet *humble himself to behold the simple* that lie *in the Dust*, and to *lift up the Poor out of the Mire*; It can be no Disparagement sure to the Greatest upon Earth, and it is a Pleasure to reflect that there are some, who think it no Disparagement to their Greatness, to give Attention to the Welfare of their Brethren, and to hearken to the Complaints of their Fellow Subjects : Who by the Influence of their high Examples, and the Weight of their Authorities, are doing God and their Country Service ; and of whom in Gratitude we therefore needs must own, that they have justly merited the publick Thanks, for the Care and Pains they have been taking for the publick Good.

The Laws of God have made this Duty of universal Extent; all Mankind are concerned in it: But they who are the Governours of Society, and are to act with the Authority of Magistrates for the Support of it, are more especially obliged to this Duty, to be *Followers of God* herein ; because it has pleased him to set a peculiar

liar Mark of Honour upon Them, in that he has called them by his own Name. *I have said*, says he by the Mouth of the Royal Prophet, that *ye are Gods*, and that *ye are all the Children of the most High:* And he said it doubtless to instruct them in their Duty, and shew them the Necessity they are under of imitating his Conduct, whose Name they bear.

These magnificent Characters, as they declare the Source from whence all their Power is derived, so do they imply the Purposes for which it ought to be employed. Nothing less could be intended by such honourable Appellations, than to point out the Obligation they are under to provide for the Prosperity of the World, and to endeavour, in Compliance with the Will of God, and the Design of their own Appointment, to render the Situation of all Persons as secure and comfortable as possible, that they may enjoy unmolested the Fruits of their own Industry, and *lead peaceable and quiet Lives in all Godliness and Honesty.* This is the original End of Government itself, and therefore ought to be the principal Aim

of

of Those, who are any way concerned in the Administration of it: Whatever Share they possess of the Publick Authority, was given them to employ for the publick Good. And when they thus fulfill the Duties of their Station, by an impartial and wise Discharge of the high Trust that is reposed in them; when with holy *Job* they can truly say, *I have put on Righteousness and it cloathed me, my Judgment is as a Robe and a Diadem;* then are they in the best and noblest Sense the *Ministers of God,* and *Children of the most High:* They do Honour to their Character, and are a publick Blessing to the Community, whereunto they belong.

This was the

Second Thing I proposed to consider: and it is a Thing that ought frequently and seriously to be considered, though it is so evident that it needs not to be proved: It ought, I say, as evident as it is, frequently to be considered, and sometimes to be inculcated upon us; because the Blessings that are constant and familiar, and those which therefore we enjoy the most, such is our Ingratitude, we are apt

apt to think of and value least. And of this kind is the Blessing of a well established Government: We, who have the Happiness of being under it, and reap the Fruits of a Regular Administration of wisely enacted Laws, can but with Difficulty conceive how miserable the Condition of Mankind would be, were there no such Laws to keep them within Bounds, and are therefore generally less sensible, than we ought to be, of the many great Advantages resulting from them. But that we may form in some sort an Idea of the wretched Effects of such a Want of Government, the Behaviour of some dissolute and abandoned Persons, which we have lately seen, and that too in a Country where they could not but have acted under some Awe of civil Justice, may serve as a kind of Specimen, to teach us what savage Creatures they would be without it: What Havock and Devastation they would make upon the Earth, were they set wholly free from the Restraint of Laws, and left to follow the Imaginations of their own evil Hearts without Hindrance or Controul.

And

And would we but sometimes consider what manifold Inconveniences all Societies must feel, where there is either no Government at all, or, which is next to none, an ill-established or an ill-administred one; the Consideration certainly would be useful, to give us a proper Sense and Relish of the Blessings we ourselves enjoy under one of the best regulated Governments in the World: A Government adorned with all the Advantages, which human Frailty will allow us to expect, and which the very meanest of its Subjects enjoy in common with those who are in the highest Stations. We are all in our Proportion Partakers of these Benefits, and therefore all have Reason to thank God, the bountiful Giver of them, and to pay with due Submission what I proposed as the

Last Thing to be considered, a proper Regard and Reverence to those, by whom as the Instruments of his Goodness he confers these Benefits upon us. ——— Nature itself instructs us that they, who discharge the difficult Functions of a State with Wisdom and Integrity, should be be highly esteemed and honoured for their Work's Sake. Which natural Instruction of undepraved Reason we also find among the positive Precepts of Revealed Religion : For by the same Authority that forbids us to speak Evil of the Rulers of the People, we are enjoined likewise to give Honour to whom Honour is due. This common and easy Tribute then, which all Men are capable of paying, they have a natural and just Right to demand of all; a Right founded upon the Principles of Reason, and ratified by Religion : and therefore to defraud them of any Part of so approved a Claim, is to transgress the Bounds both of Decency and Duty.

There is nothing in the World is more generally agreed in, than the Necessity of Government to obtain the Ends of Society. It was the Desire of Mutual Preservation and Defence, of Protection against Wrong and Robbery, and the secure Possession of their private Properties, that was the first Inducement to Mankink to unite themselves together in distinct Societies: that they might fit every Man

Man in Quietness under their own Vine, and enjoy safely the Fruits of their own Labour. But these, as all other Blessings and Benefits, are the Gifts of God; and Governours are the Ministers appointed by him, through whom he derives those Blessings and Benefits to the World: So that the Peace and Prosperity of Nations is owing principally, under God, to the wise Care and Conduct of their Rulers, and the prudent Administration of Government therein. Without this, all those intolerable Mischiefs must ensue, which Men's unrestrained Appetites and Passions would produce, and which unavoidably break the Bands, and are the sure Destruction of all Societies.

It is not to be expected that all the Individuals of any Community should universally agree, as to the exact Bounds and Extent of Civil Power, any more than it is, that all the different Communities throughout the World should pursue the same System, and frame their Governments upon the same Plan: But without a due Regard and Reverence paid to those Persons, who are entrusted with the

the Management of publick Affairs, and a dutiful Submission to their legal Authority, the best contrived Constitutions in the World could not answer the Ends of their Establishment, nor could any of the Purposes of Life be effectually served by them.——But farther,

Every high Place of Trust and Power has its Burthens, as well as Honours, that are inseparable from it; and the Magistrate of Justice, from the very Nature of his Office, must have his Share: He cannot in the Course of Things but incur great Enmity, and provoke all the Outrage and Resentment of evil Doers, if he be resolute in performing faithfully the Duty of his Station, and endeavouring, as that Duty obliges him, *to break the Jaws of the Wicked, and pluck the Spoil out of his Teeth.* One would think then that a Sense of Gratitude should inspire every generous Mind with an Esteem and Reverence for those who bear the Weight of so important an Employment, as the Administration of publick Justice, and the Execution of the Laws of a Kingdom. And it appears indeed to to have been the Wisdom of all Nations to treat their Characters with the most particular Regard: For from hence, 'tis probable, arose the Practice, now in universal Use, of appropriating to Magistrates external Marks of Splendour and Distinction; that by the Distance naturally created, in the Minds of the People, by the outward Ensigns of Dignity annexed to their Office, the Reverence due to their Persons might be properly preserved, and their Authority thereby maintained and upheld.——But lest this should fail of its Effect, and the Principle of Gratitude not have Force sufficient to secure the Practice of this Duty, the Holy Scriptures have bound it upon us by all possible Obligations.

There are no Duties that our Blessed Saviour in the Institution of his Laws had a greater Regard to, than those which arise from Civil Society, and tend to make us useful Members of the Community to which we belong. Accordingly as he laid the best Foundation for such a general Practice of Truth and Justice, as, if duly followed, would secure effectually

tually the Properties of private Persons; so he was particularly careful to save the Rights of Princes, and recommended in the strongest Terms that Obedience which is due to those, whom the Laws have appointed Rulers in every Nation. And altho', when the *Jews* maliciously accused him of Treason against the State, and impeached him before *Pilate* as an Enemy to *Cæsar* for declaring himself a King, he does not deny that he was a King, because, as he tells us, it was *for this End he was born, that he might bear Witness to that Truth*; yet to shew that he had no evil Designs against the Person of *Cæsar*, nor any Intention of interfering either with his, or any human Government whatsoever, he expressly asserts that his *Kingdom was not of this World.* And again, that the Rulers of the World might have no reasonable Grounds of Prejudice, no Enmity against him or his Religion, through any Apprehension of Danger from them to their respective Governments, he enjoins it as an indispensable Duty upon all his Followers, to *render unto* Cæsar *the Things that are* Cæsar's, as well as

unto

unto God the things that are God's. They, indeed, who are invested with the supreme Authority, and act as God's immediate Vicegerents in the World, are the persons, in Respect of whom this Injunction was particularly given, but it may very fairly be extended likewise, under due Restrictions, to all that are commissioned under it, and have any Share of that Authority delegated to them.

Such then is the Doctrine of the Christian Religion, as taught by the great Author and Founder of it, *Jesus Christ* himself. And his Apostles, who followed him in the uniform Practice of all those Virtues, by which Societies subsist, have both by their Precept and Example taught us the same Thing.———St. *Paul* in his Epistle to the *Romans*, speaking of a Christian's Duty to the Civil Magistrate, commands that *every Soul be subject to the higher Powers :* And deduces our Obligation to this Duty from these two Considerations. First, that it is the Will of God: For *there is no Power*, he tells us, *but of God ; the Powers* in being *are ordained* of him: it must therefore, as he then

then concludes, be the indispensable Duty of all Subjects to obey; because if they *resist*, they *resist the Ordinance of God*. The other Consideration is taken from the general Design of Government, which shews it to be our Interest, as well as Duty, to be obedient Subjects: that *he is the Minister of God* to us *for Good*; and that therefore in regard to ourselves we should submit to his Authority, *not only for Wrath, but also for Conscience Sake*; as being truly sensible of the Advantages of Government, that it is the *Ordinance of God*, for the *Good* of Mankind. And as an Explication of this Duty of Subjection to the higher Powers, and to teach us the Extent of our Obedience to it, St. *Peter* requires our Submission, not only to the supreme Magistrate himself, but also to all, in their Degree and Proportion, who are invested with publick Authority: *Submit yourselves*, says he, *to every Ordinance of Man for the Lord's Sake, whether it be to the King as Supreme, or unto Governours, as unto them that are sent by him, for the Punishment of evil Doers, and for the Praise of them that do well.*

Now

Now these Scriptures, as they instruct us in our Behaviour towards the Persons of Magistrates, so do they teach us likewise the great Expediency and Usefulness of Magistracy itself, and shews us the Grounds and Reasons of its Institution: They inform us that Magistrates were appointed to be the Guardians of the publick Quiet, and had the *Sword* of Justice put into their Hands for this very Purpose, *to execute Wrath upon him that doeth Evil.* And it is a melancholy Truth, which I can only publish and lament, that never was the Vigilance and Courage of the Civil Magistrate more necessary, than in these evil Days into which we are fallen: when, to say nothing of the private Vices that abound amongst us, an almost general Licentiousness is practised throughout the Kingdom, against both the the common Reason and common Interest of Mankind, and in defiance of all Authority, whether sacred or civil.

This is the unavoidable Consequence of that Contempt of Religion, which is so prevalent in this degenerate Age. Men have

have been so accustoming themselves to look with Scorn upon every thing relating to it, that scarce any Appearance of the Reverence due to the Supreme Being is preserved amongst us They deride the very Notion of a wise and good God, that made and governs all Things, and in Consequence treat the Duty of attending upon his Worship, as at best but a Matter of great Indifference, whether it be observed, or no. How much the Influence and Example of some of high Rank and Condition in the World have contributed to the Propagation of these pernicious Notions, will best be left to their Consideration, in whose Power it is to stop it : But however that may be, this every Body sees; that this contemptuous Impiety is got to a prodigious Height, and has overspread, in an uncommon Manner, all Sorts of People. And when this is the Case, when the Subjects of any Kingdom have thrown off all Regard to God, so as to be kept no longer within the Bounds of Duty by the Fear of divine Justice, what is there left that can procure their Obedience to earthly Rulers, or hinder

hinder them from *walking every one in the evil Imagination of their own Hearts,* from doing *Evil,* and that *continually*? Take away Religion, and the Obligation which it lays upon us to Obedience, and all human Authority must fall to the Ground. This is so apparently true, that it has been the constant Practice of the wisest Politicians in all Ages, to use their utmost Endeavours to preserve Religion, as judging it to be the only Thing that could preserve Them. And their Judgment was well grounded: For when once Religion has lost its Influence upon the Minds of Men, and they are come to *have no Fear of God before their Eyes,* what can prevent them, upon this Supposition, from endeavouring to get loose from the Restraints of Government, and, whenever they can do it safely, throwing off their Allegiance to those whom they have no Mind should be Rulers over them?

The Rights of Princes must, in different Nations, be as different as the Laws themselves are, upon which they are founded: But be they what they will, the

the Claim they have to them is of divine Original, and derived ultimately from Him, who is the *Governour among the Nations ; who ruleth in the Kingdom of Men, and giveth it to whomsoever he will.* As long therefore as Men retain in their Minds such a Sense of God, as disposes them to give Him his Right, they will probably not fail of giving *Cæsar* his: But whenever it happens that the divine Authority is disregarded, and God himself, and his Laws neglected, it cannot be any Wonder that the Commands of Men should be lightly esteemed. These loose and irreligious Notions then we may fairly fix upon, as one principal Cause of that Depravity of Manners, which so thrives and spreads amongst us: that having first by their Influence been divested of the Fear of God, we are come at length to have no Regard for Man. *Presumptuous* are we, *and self-willed,* and like that profligate and abandoned People described by the Apostle, *we despise Dominions, and are not afraid to speak Evil of Dignities.* What will be the Issue of this growing Evil, or where the End of
these

these Things will be, God only knows, who is the Disposer of all Events: That some Care should be taken to stop its Progress, a prudential Concern for our own Safety, had we no other Inducements, renders absolutely necessary. But there are Motives of a higher Nature; the Regard we have for our Religion, Laws, and Liberties, should excite us to it; as an effectual Means to promote the Glory of God, and to secure the Peace of the Kingdom.——— And happy is it for us, that we have some illustrious Instances of Persons, who have Concern enough for both, to engage in their Behalf: and to give us Hopes however, that by this their seasonable Zeal in *doing Justice and Judgment,* they may be able, with the Blessing of Almighty God, if not to correct all the Abuses of these daring and outrageous People, at least to give a Check to their Insolence, and keep them within modest Bounds: that those, who will not be perswaded by the Mercy of an indulgent Sovereign, to pay him willingly that Submission which the very Design of Government gives an undoubted Right to, to, a just Severity may restrain from such enormous Practices, as bring Disgrace and Danger to Government itself.

Let us then humbly request of God, that as he has now begun to make us happy, by settling us in a State of Peace, and putting away all Fear of Danger from our Enemies abroad, he would go on to the Completion of it, by repressing our Disorders at Home. That so we, who are blessed with a wise and well-constituted Government, administred by a mild and most gracious Prince, may testify our Sense and Worthiness of so great a Blessing, by living peaceably and quietly under it: That to the Fervency of our Prayers we may add our Endeavours likewise to preserve an Establishment, which is the only Means, under God, of preserving us : And in a Word, which is the common Dictate both of Reason and Religion, that all, who share in the Benefits, may join in the Duties of an obedient People.

F I N I S.